The
Middle
School
Rules of
SKYLAR DIGGINS

as told by
Sean Jensen

Illustrated by Daniel Smith

BroadStreet
PUBLISHING

BroadStreet Publishing Group LLC
Racine, Wisconsin, USA
broadstreetpublishing.com

Middle School Rules of Skylar Diggins

ISBN 978-1-4245-5244-3 (hard cover)
ISBN 978-1-4245-5245-0 (e-book)

Illustrated by Daniel Smith | sonsoftyce.com
Cover and interior design by Garborg Design Works | garborgdesign.com
Editorial services provided by Ginger Garrett | gingergarrett.com
and Michelle Winger | literallyprecise.com

Printed in China.

16 17   18   19   20   21   22   7   6   5   4   3   2   1

ACKNOWLEDGMENTS
from Skylar Diggins

I want to thank my family and my parents: Mom, Daddymoe, Daddy, and Shay.
Mom, you are my role model. Thank for being a great example.
Daddymoe, thanks for always believing in me.

Neefah, Destyn, June, Tayta – I love you all so much and I am
so proud of you! I can't wait to see what your futures hold.

Thank you to my amazing grandparents for always being there.
I will always cherish our moments together!

Thank you to my Notre Dame family, especially Coach McGraw and Niele.
Coach, thank you for giving me an incredible opportunity to play at the next level.
Niele, thank you for being a great mentor. Thank you both for looking out
for me off the court, challenging me on the court, and always pushing me
outside my comfort zone.

Daniel, thank you for being one of my biggest supporters. I love you.

To my shugs, Em and Ash, thanks for always being great friends and sisters.

I want to thank all of my teammates. I've crossed paths with a lot of people
through basketball and each team in every phase of my life was special
in its own way. You helped push me.

Finally, the city of South Bend, my home, thank you.

from Sean Jensen

First, I give praise to God for all He has done in my life.

I want thank my wife Erica for her love,

and my kids, Elijah and Zarah, for inspiring me.

I also want to thank Roc Nation Sports, especially Joe Branch and Jana
Fleishman, for providing myself and my publisher the connection to Skylar Diggins.

Lastly, I want to thank Daniel, Skylar, and her family for trusting me
to tell their story.

INTRODUCTION

Dear Reader,

Many of you look up to me and other professional athletes. Many of you wear our jerseys and wait in long lines for our autographs.

But I want you to know something: I was that kid too.

That's why I wanted to do *The Middle School Rules*. People either forget or even make up my story. They see the end product but ignore the path to get there.

You don't know someone's story until you see it through their eyes and hear it from their mouth.

This is *my* story.

I was a little girl from South Bend, and my dream was so simple but so big. I wanted to play basketball at Notre Dame and then in the WNBA.

I did both of those things, but I didn't do it alone.

My family comes from a lot of different cultures and places. They taught me precious lessons. The stories of my life happened with the most important people of my life. Each time I read this book, I go back to those special moments. It's something that's evergreen for me, something that I want to pass along to my children.

These family stories are essential to me becoming the Skylar I am today.

I wanted to play at Notre Dame, but I didn't know I would get to be a captain, go to three Final Fours, develop amazing friendships, and earn a business degree.

I wanted to play basketball, but I didn't know I would travel the world, playing in China, Thailand, Argentina, and Greece, among many other places, and meet lifelong friends.

In the WNBA, I've even played with some of the women I looked up to, like Tamika Catchings and Diana Taurasi, among others.

I've done so many things I never thought I would be able to do.

No matter what you want to do, you have to be willing to put in the work to get there. You can do anything, no matter who you are and what your background is.

Skylar Diggins

FOREWORD

It was August 1993, and Skylar had just celebrated her third birthday at Hardee's. I did not attend the party, but I was going to meet her for the first time afterward. I was very nervous. I had been dating her mom Renee for about four months, and I had heard so many stories about Skylar that I felt I knew her.

When they got out of Renee's black Nissan Sentra, I saw this beautiful little girl who looked just like her mom. As Renee started to introduce me, I abruptly said, "Hi Skylar, I'm Maurice!" She looked at me, stepped closer to her Mom, and just waved. I immediately knew it was going to be a challenge. I started to think about how I was going to develop a relationship with little Sky and how I would be there for her, to love her and teach her, and help guide her through life as if she were my own.

Here's the thing: Skylar ended up teaching me so much, and loving me even more. It's one of her gifts. In all of her life lessons as a youngster, she always took away the positive things she could use to better herself and the people around her.

As one of the most competitive people I have ever been around, Skylar is also loyal, thoughtful, caring, honest, and genuine. She's not the tallest athlete I've ever coached. Or the fastest. And I've coached many great ball players—but Skylar was the hardest working. Her effort applies to everything she does, on and off the court. The one thing that makes her the most special is that she makes everyone around her better: her teammates, coaches, fans, and even opponents!

The Middle School Rules of Skylar Diggins is about Sky's life. You will get to know her family and friends, but most of all you will get to know her and what an awesome person she is.

There's good, there's great, there's special, and then there's Skylar!

Coach Moe Scott
Skylar's DaddyMoe

TABLE OF CONTENTS

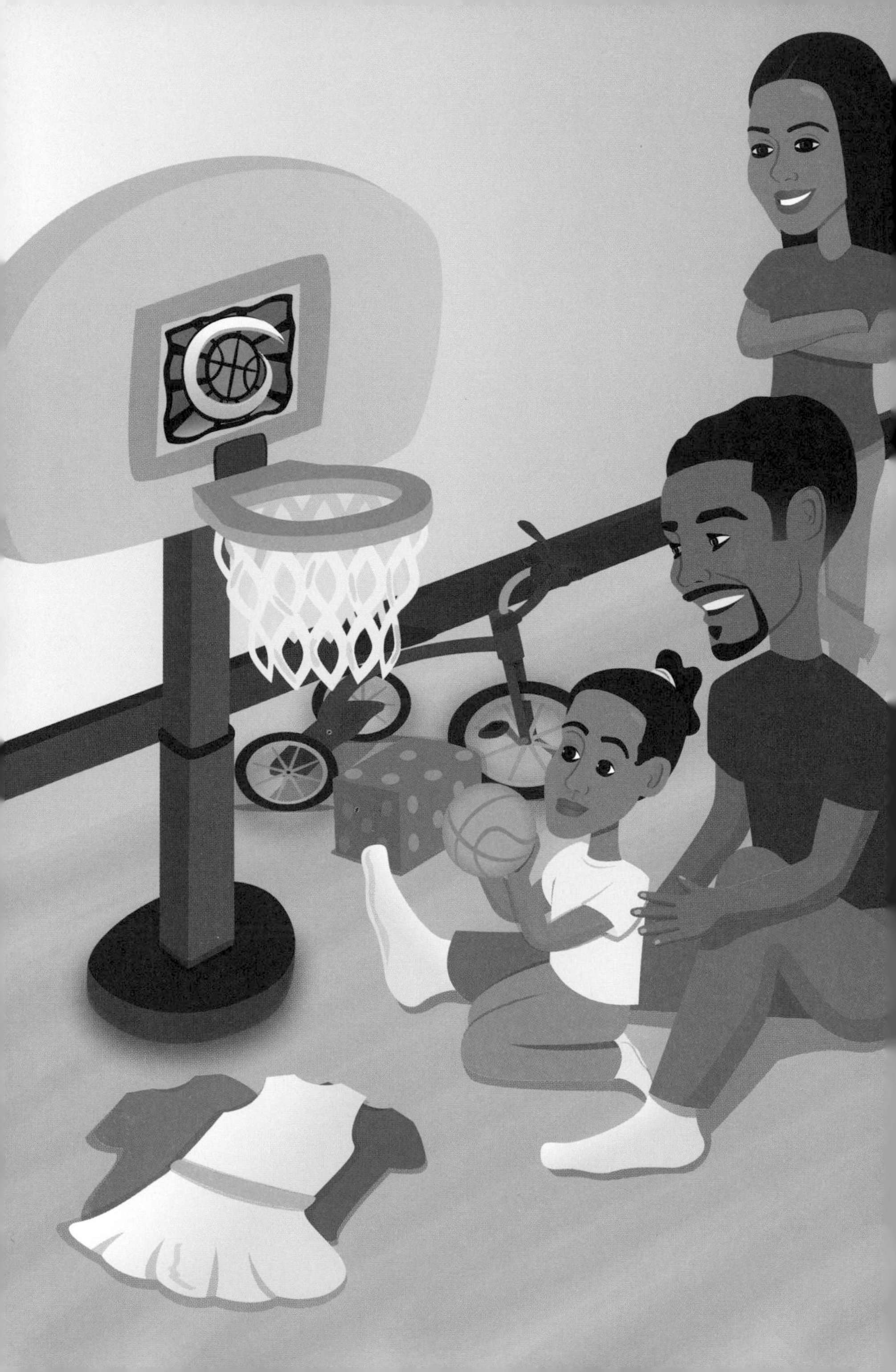

Chapter 1

Starting Early

All birthdays are special, and the best o[illegible]ring great memories and presents. But sometimes a p[illegible]nt creates a memory *and* changes your life.

Skylar sees a stack of wrapped gift[illegible]he third house on the "Skylar Diggins Birthday Tour." It'[illegible]ust 2, 1993, and she is celebrating her third birthday. [illegible]as so many aunties and uncles and grandparents that s[illegible]s her way around South Bend, Indiana, from home to [illegible], collecting hugs, kisses, and gifts.

At her first stop, she [illegible]ives a soft and cuddly Barney-the-dinosaur doll. Now, at G[illegible]y Pauline and Granddad Bennie's, she sees gifts: a red tricycle with a red bow, and then, a few feet away, one massive box wrapped in blue paper.

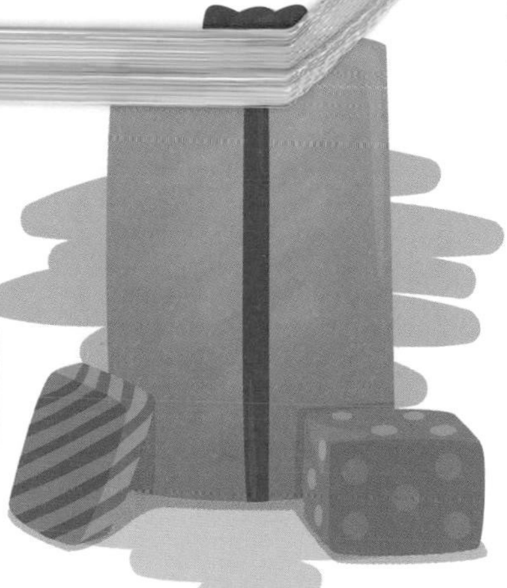

Her eyes light up.

How could this day get any better? she thinks.

"That's from Mom and Daddy," her daddy says.

Her mom, Renee, however, rolls her eyes. Mom has no idea what's in the big box.

FLASHBACK

Tige is Skylar's daddy, and he played two years of varsity basketball at Clay High School. He still plays in very competitive rec leagues. He loves to watch sports, especially supporting teams from the University of Michigan.

The college's mascot is the Wolverine, and Tige tracks a lot of their games, especially in football. Once, when he was feeding baby Skylar a bottle of milk, the Wolverines scored a touchdown, and he jumped up and screamed, "Yeah!"

Startled, baby Skylar cries.

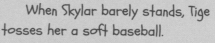

When Skylar barely stands, Tige tosses her a soft baseball.

She catches it.

When Skylar barely moves, Tige hands her a football.

She runs with it.

"She's kind of athletic at two years old," Tige proudly tells his friends.

When he playfully tries to tackle her, Skylar does all she can to avoid him and keeps running with the ball.

Renee does not like this sort of horse play one bit.

"She's not a boy!" she yells at Tige. "You're too physical with her."

Mom nervously watches as Skylar rips the wrapping paper off the present that's bigger than the three-year-old.

Pictured on the massive box is a basketball hoop.

Skylar squeals with delight.

"Open it!" Skylar shouts, jumping up and down. "Open it, please!"

The hoop has a black base, a silver pole that adjusts height, an orange rim with a thick, white net, and a black backboard with a basketball pictured in an orange border.

Daddy quickly puts the hoop together, filling the black base with water so it won't topple over.

Once the hoop is assembled, Skylar picks up the mini orange basketball and shoots it.

Swish!

She makes her first attempt.

Skylar feels a tingling sensation rush through her body. She *loves* the feeling.

"Skylar, why don't you open up your other gifts?" Mom gently asks, pointing to a half dozen wrapped boxes.

But Skylar just wants to play with her new hoop.

She trots over to her Daddy, prodding him to pick her up so she can dunk the ball.

"Let's play," she says.

Daddy immediately adjusts the hoop to its tallest setting, which is six feet high. Skylar tries another shot, but it's not so

and she often misses the rim altogether.

When the game starts, Daddy doesn't take it easy on Skylar.

"Get that out of here!" he playfully shouts as he sends Skylar's shot flying across the room.

Skylar furrows her eyebrows, and Mom shakes her head.

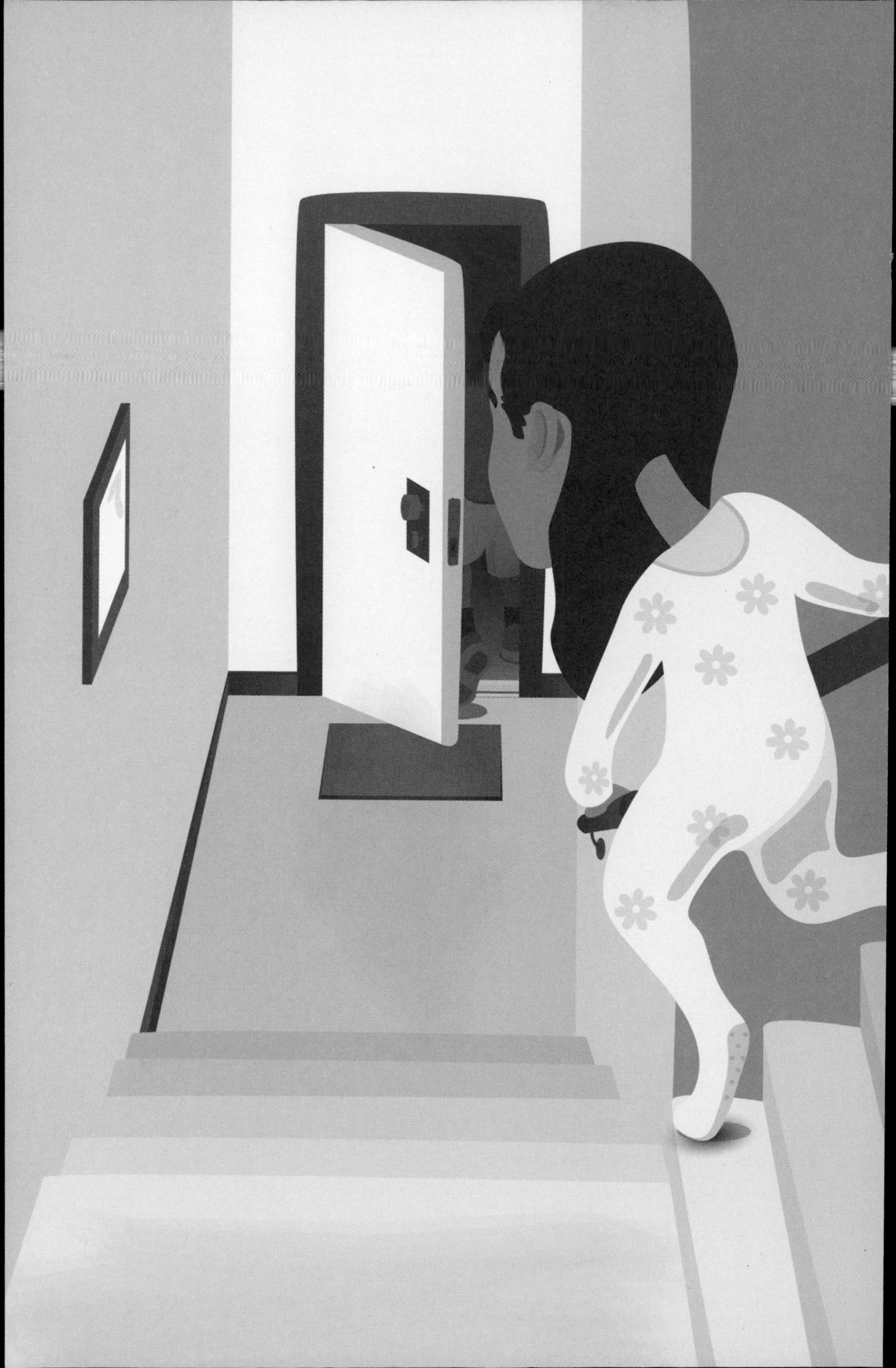

Chapter 2 Meeting Maurice

Skylar loves both of her parents, and her parents love her.

Tige and Renee met in high school at ShowBiz Pizza Place, a chain restaurant that features arcade games and coin-operated rides.

While Renee was pregnant, a family friend from the east coast came for a visit. The woman was pretty and smart, and her name was Skyler. So, when Renee and Tige discovered in early 1990 that they were having a girl, Tige suggested Skylar—with an *a* instead of an *e*—as the baby's name.

Renee loved it.

But Skylar's mom and dad don't stay together. Mom and Skylar live in a two-bedroom apartment just east of South Bend, in the [illegible] new man into Skylar's life after her third birthday. His name is Maurice, and basketball is a big part of his life too. He plays, coaches, and even referees the sport. Maurice works at the Martin Luther King Jr. Recreation Center on

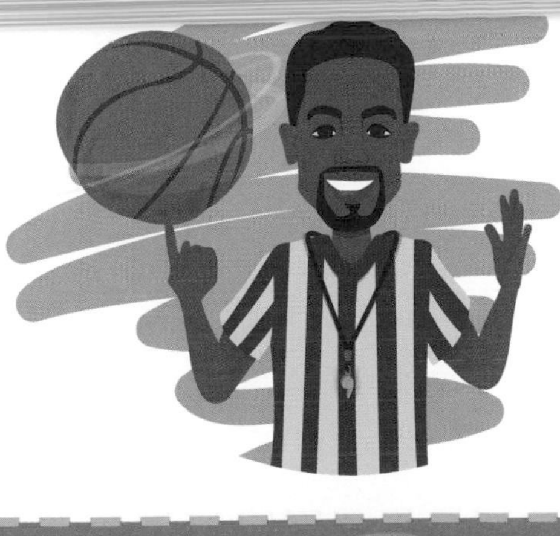

the west side of South Bend, a few blocks away from the city cemetery.

Skylar does not like Maurice. She figures *he* is the reason Mom and Daddy are not together.

After the King Center closes in the evening, Maurice sometimes stops by the Mishawaka apartment to chat and watch television with Mom. Though she is supposed to be in bed asleep, Skylar sometimes makes a point of walking from her bedroom to the top of the stairs.

"Is *he* gone yet?" she yells down.

But as she starts to spend more time at the King Center, Skylar notices something about Maurice. People love him—especially kids! He pours himself into all of them: the big ones, little ones, disabled ones, talented ones, and not-so-talented ones.

Maurice is patient, energetic, and he makes everything fun.

After a while, Skylar doesn't like it when other kids want to give Maurice a hug or a hi-five. Slowly but surely, her heart softens toward him. She admires his personality, and he makes her laugh—a lot.

She simply could not, *not* like him!

When Skylar is six, she learns from Mom and Maurice that they plan to get married. Maurice pulls Skylar aside.

"How do you feel about this, Skylar?" he gently asks.

She appreciates that Maurice is thoughtful enough to talk to her *before* the marriage.

"I'm happy for you, Maurice!" Skylar says.

Maurice smiles.

"Let's come up with another name for you to call me," Maurice says. "Call me whatever makes you comfortable. Why don't you think about it for a while."

What would she call this man? She already has a daddy.

After a few days, Skylar comes up with the right name.

"Can I call you Daddymoe?" she asks Maurice. Skylar likes the name because it combines his nickname with his budding role in her life.

"Sure," he says with his big smile. "That's got a nice ring to it."

Skylar likes the name more and more because *she* is the only one that calls Maurice Daddymoe. And as time passes, people only use the name in relation to her. For example, a relative would say to Skylar, "Where is your Daddymoe?"

There's another advantage to opening up her heart to Daddymoe; he has a daughter named Haneefah who is two years younger than Skylar.

Now I'm not the only child, Skylar thinks. *This is amazing!*

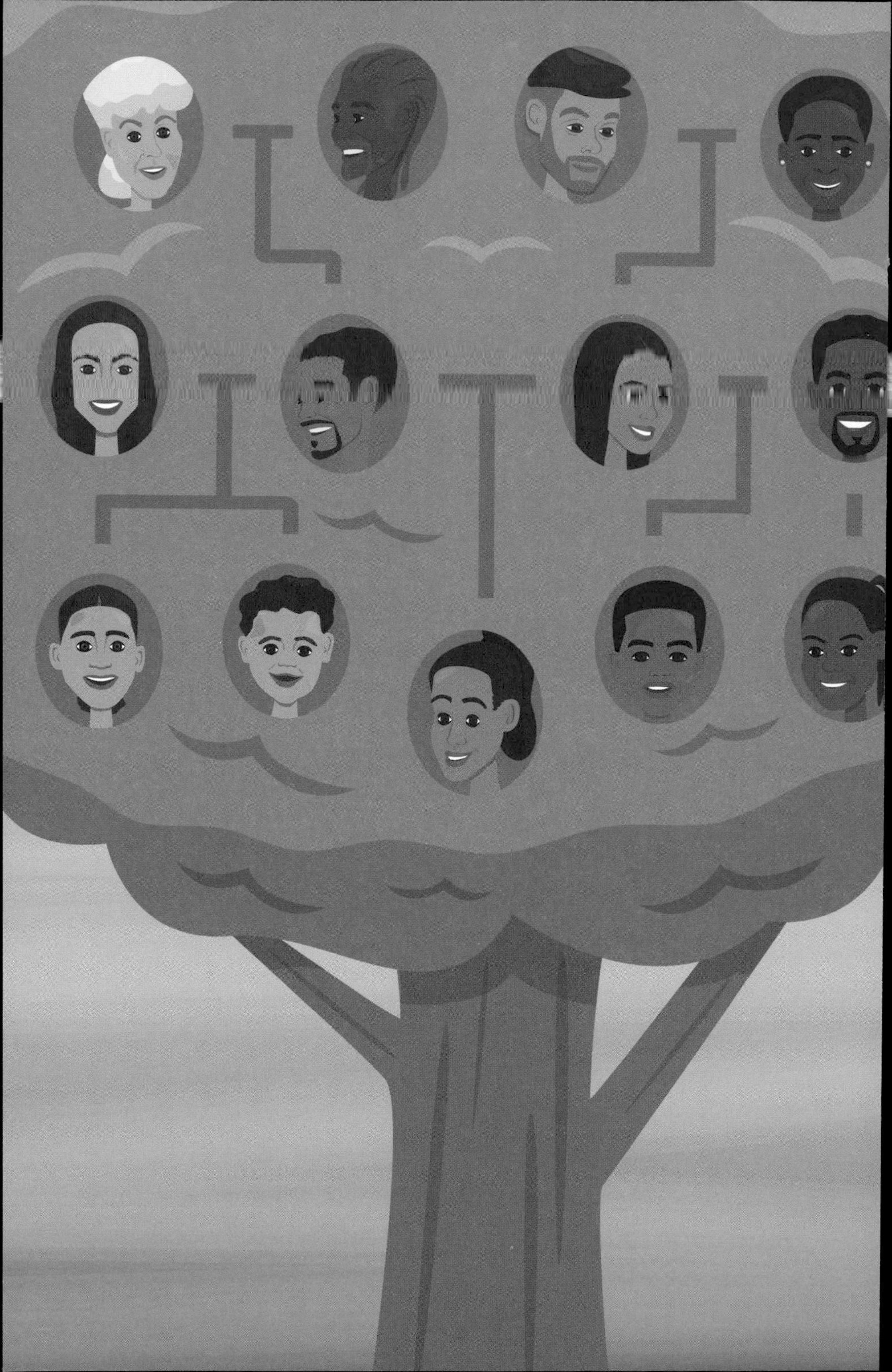

Chapter 3

Black or White

Daddymoe provides another strong branch in Skylar's family tree. Mom's parents both remarry as well, which gives Skylar two additional older, wiser adults in her life. More grandparents to guide and care for her.

Skylar feels very fortunate to have so many people that love her.

A large number of strangers coming together can sometimes complicate situations. But all the adults in Skylar's life agree on an important point: their individual differences don't matter; the one

Skylar and her family don't dwell on their *diversity:* meaning each person's racial background. When she is in first grade, Skylar looks at a signup sheet that asks her to identify herself by race.

Black or white? Skylar reads on the paper. *Well, most of my family is black, but my Granny Pauline is white, so I'm both.*

She holds the pencil with no eraser over the paper.

Should she ignore the question? Or mark black or white?

How could I squeeze everything I am into a simple box? she thinks.

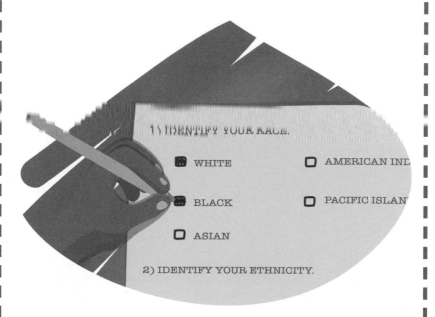

1) IDENTIFY YOUR RACE.

☒ WHITE   ☐ AMERICAN IND

☒ BLACK   ☐ PACIFIC ISLAN

☐ ASIAN

2) IDENTIFY YOUR ETHNICITY.

Skylar puts the pencil to paper and checks both boxes.
What does it matter? she thinks.
It does not matter to her.
But, Skylar realizes, it does to others.
For many years, blacks and whites have had problems getting along in South Bend.
The city got its name because it's near the southernmost "bend" of the St. Joseph River, which was important to the early settlers in the 1800s. The University of Notre Dame, a world-famous Catholic college, was established in 1842 in the northern part of town. A decade later, the first big company arrived: a car manufacturer named after the Studebaker brothers.

In the 1960s, some people didn't like that Granddad Bennie, who was 6 feet 9 inches and black, was married to Granny Pauline who was white.

When Tige was a little boy, one white man with a knife and another with a crowbar approached Granddad's truck at a stop light.

Granddad sped away before the two men did anything.

Granny Pauline, though, is always so calm and cool.

As Skylar grows older, she notices many puzzled looks

Outside the grocery store, one white woman approaches Granny Pauline and asks her, "Who is this child you're with?"

"That's my granddaughter," Granny Pauline says confidently with a smile.

The woman frowns and walks away.

Granny Pauline leans in toward Skylar.

Granny Pauline's Rule

"Sweetie, accept everybody," Granny Pauline says. "You can be friends with anybody no matter what they look like or what their past is. Don't prejudge others."

Skylar sees how in love Granny Pauline and Granddad Bennie are, the kindness they show one another: how Granddad Bennie always opens the door for Granny, and how she always gives him the last bite of cake. Their love is deep, particularly since others sometimes make unkind comments about them in public or give them dirty looks.

They teach her how to tune out negative people and handle a bad situation.

On weekends and holidays, Skylar spends a lot of time with Granny Pauline and Granddad Bennie, but she also visits a lot of relatives. She gets to know many of them in her early years because both her parents have unpredictable work schedules. For a while, Skylar's mother works as a flight attendant, and she sometimes travels on nights or weekends.

This means Skylar's grandparents help care for her and transport her to school and activities. It isn't uncommon for Skylar to have 30 people at her games and events!

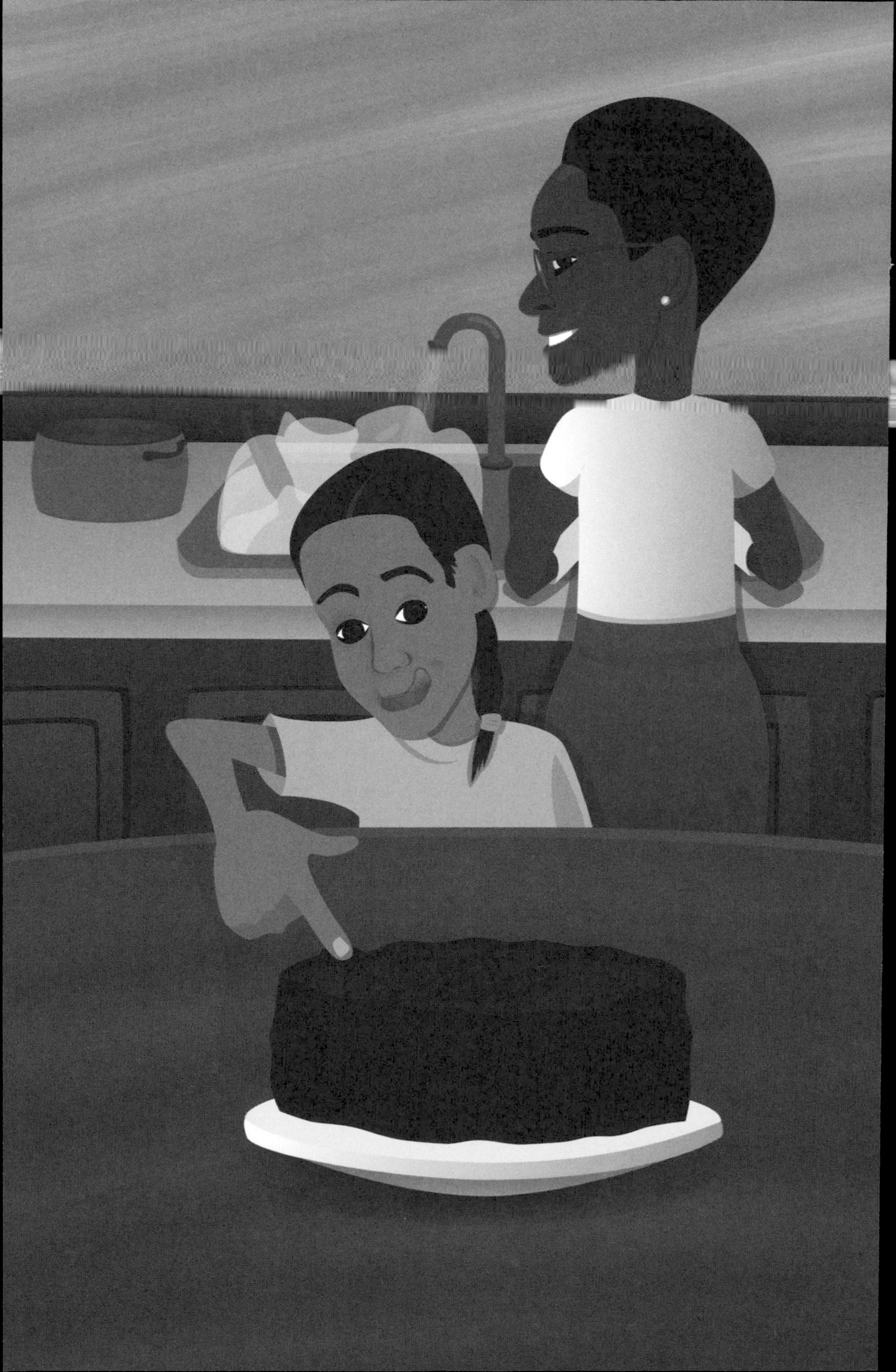

Chapter 4

Granny Stella

As a little girl, Skylar spends the most time at her Granny Stella and Grandpa Harold's house, which is close to Skylar's elementary school.

Granny Stella is always at home, tending to her garden, cleaning her white house with green shutters, and cooking everything from scratch in her kitchen.

Granny Stella is from Starkville, Mississippi, and she is as sweet as her famous sweet potato pie. She does not believe in strangers—anyone who walks through her front door is a friend and deserves a home-cooked meal.

stove. It's dangerous for a child that age to cook but that's what her family needed from Stella. Being an obedient child, she didn't question her mom about anything.

By eight, Stella was responsible for cooking all her family's meals.

Because she has been cooking for so long, Stella instinctively knows where every spoon, straw, pot, and small appliance is in the kitchen. She never uses a recipe or a measuring cup.

"A little of this, a little of that," Granny says, "and a pinch of this, baby. That's all you need!"

Granny Stella does not need air fresheners, like flowers or spices, which make a room smell nice. Enter her home, and delicious aromas greet you: cakes, breads, soups, main courses like fried chicken, and side dishes like mac and cheese.

But Skylar loves Granny's lemon cakes!

If she smells lemon cakes upon entering the house, Skylar runs toward the kitchen and yells, "This one's mine, this one's mine!"

If you don't claim one, someone else surely does.

The one smell Skylar does not like is *chitterlings*. Also known as *chitlins*, it is the intestines of a pig, and boiling them in water helps clean them.

Granny makes buckets of chitlins at a time, so the smell overpowers the entire house. Skylar tries to spend as much time in the yard on days Granny cooks chitlins.

But in general, Skylar likes to help Granny in the kitchen, especially when *collard greens* are being made. A staple of "soul

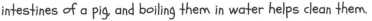

greens are a leafy vegetable that come in bunches.

Preparing collard greens requires a lot of time and energy. Skylar helps Granny "pick the greens," which means she uses her hands to take the dark green leaf off the hard, light green stalk.

Skylar and Granny sit at the kitchen table, with bunches upon bunches of unpicked collard greens. Skylar likes the work, but she *loves* the conversation.

Granny tells Skylar about growing up in Starkville in the 1930s and 1940s.

In 1929, the Great Depression started in the United States and impacted the world economy. People stopped spending money, products piled up and the value of stocks—a share of a company—decreased at a record rate.

All Americans struggled but black Americans, especially those in the South, struggled the most. By 1932, 50 percent of black Americans were unemployed: that is twice as much as the American average. Stella candidly shares the positive and negative stories of her childhood.

Given her experience, Granny Stella always has the same message for Skylar.

Granny Stella's Rule

"It's your dream, Sky," Granny Stella says. "It's not mine; it's not your mom's. Follow *your* dream, and know that Granny loves you."

After that message, Granny hugs Skylar, wrapping her arms around her tight.

"Hug like you mean it," Granny whispers.

Skylar never gets tired of that talk. It makes her feel like she can do *anything*.

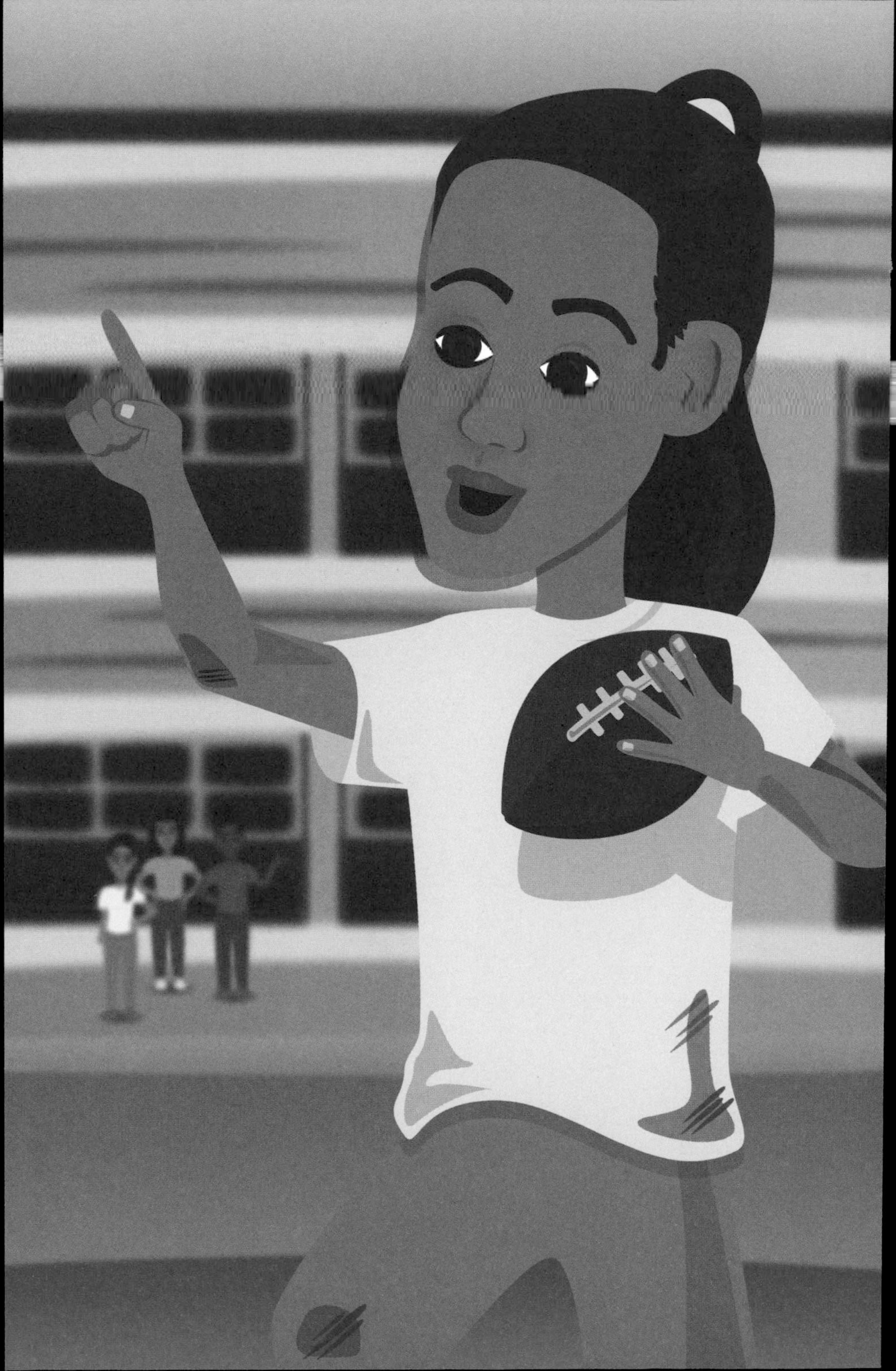

Chapter 5

Rough Around the Edges

Skylar also likes Granny Stella and Grandpa Harold's house because there are always kids around. Cousins Harry, Richmond, Rhonda, and Brannon are regulars.

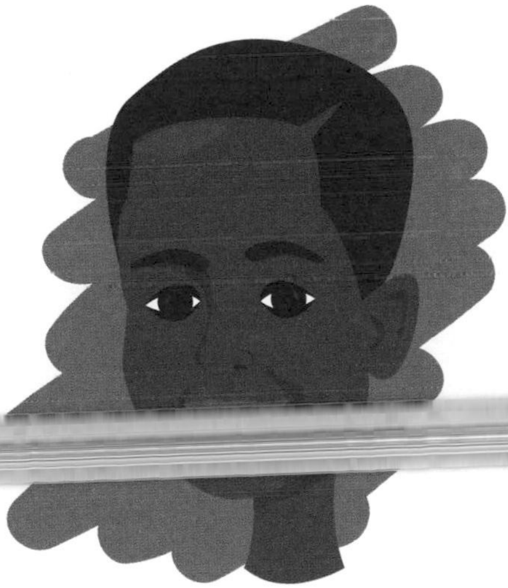

But her favorite cousin is Leland, who is two years older than Skylar. They just click.

All the kids love Granny's [illegible] and snacks, like Little Debbie cakes. They can watch cartoons or play board games.

But Skylar likes to be on the move, and Leland is the one she can usually coax into joining her.

Granny often stays in the kitchen. When Skylar and Leland run through the house, they know what Granny will say.

"Be careful. You'll make the cake fall!"

Usually, though, Skylar wants to play in the backyard. There are flowers, healthy green grass, and a garden with tomatoes and collard greens, all surrounded by a white fence.

Skylar uses her imagination to turn the space into many things: a wrestling ring, basketball court, and a field for football, kickball, or baseball.

On the right side of the house is a tall thorn bush. They call it "Spike," and it swallows up balls of every kind.

"You hit it, you get it!"

When they play baseball, a butterfly lawn decoration is first base and the thorn bush is third base. A home run goes over the white fence.

Skylar hits *a lot* of balls over the fence.

"Not again," Leland says, as Skylar blasts another hit over it.

Leland is laid back and not overly competitive. Although he's older and bigger, he recognizes how competitive Skylar is about everything. She never backs down, especially in contact sports.

When they wrestle, Skylar bucks and squirms, refusing to let Leland pin her. When they play football, Skylar bounces up after someone runs her over.

Skylar is tough. But she is also clumsy.

When kids run, Skylar is the one who usually falls.

She scrapes up her knees, drawing blood, and then runs inside the house. Every time, Granny is waiting. She dabs cotton swabs

dipped in peroxide to clean the small cuts, slides on a Band-Aid, and then sends Skylar back to Leland and the others.

Skylar's mom does not like the rough play though.

FLASHBACK

Mom signs Skylar up for ballet at three, but Skylar does not like leotards, tights, and slippers. She'd rather ~~be~~ ~~tapping~~ her feet to the hyped beat of the latest song, not standing on her tippy-toes to the slow rhythm of classics from centuries ago.

Besides, ballet hurts her feet!

Skylar tells her mom she's done with ballet after two sessions.

"Why don't you try it a little longer?" Mom asks.

"I tried it, Mom," Skylar says. "But I really, really don't like it."

Mom's Rule

"Try everything," Mom says. "You never know what your niche is going to be."

Mom signs Skylar up for cheerleading, swimming, gymnastics, tennis, and soccer.

None interest Skylar.

In first grade, during recess, the girls talk or play hopscotch. Skylar, meanwhile, plays basketball and football with the boys. In both sports, Skylar likes the ball in her hands. She's the point guard in basketball and the quarterback in football.

The boys like playing with Skylar because she is a good shooter and a good passer, throwing a tight spiral.

The other girls do not approve.

"What is wrong with her?" Jennifer says to Angie. "Look how dirty she's getting!"

Skylar wonders why the other girls don't want to play too. It's so much fun!

Many days, Skylar comes home from school with holes in the knees of her pants, and with streaks of dirt on her face and arms.

Mom shakes her head.

Skylar grins and kisses her on the cheek before she heads to the bathroom to clean herself up.

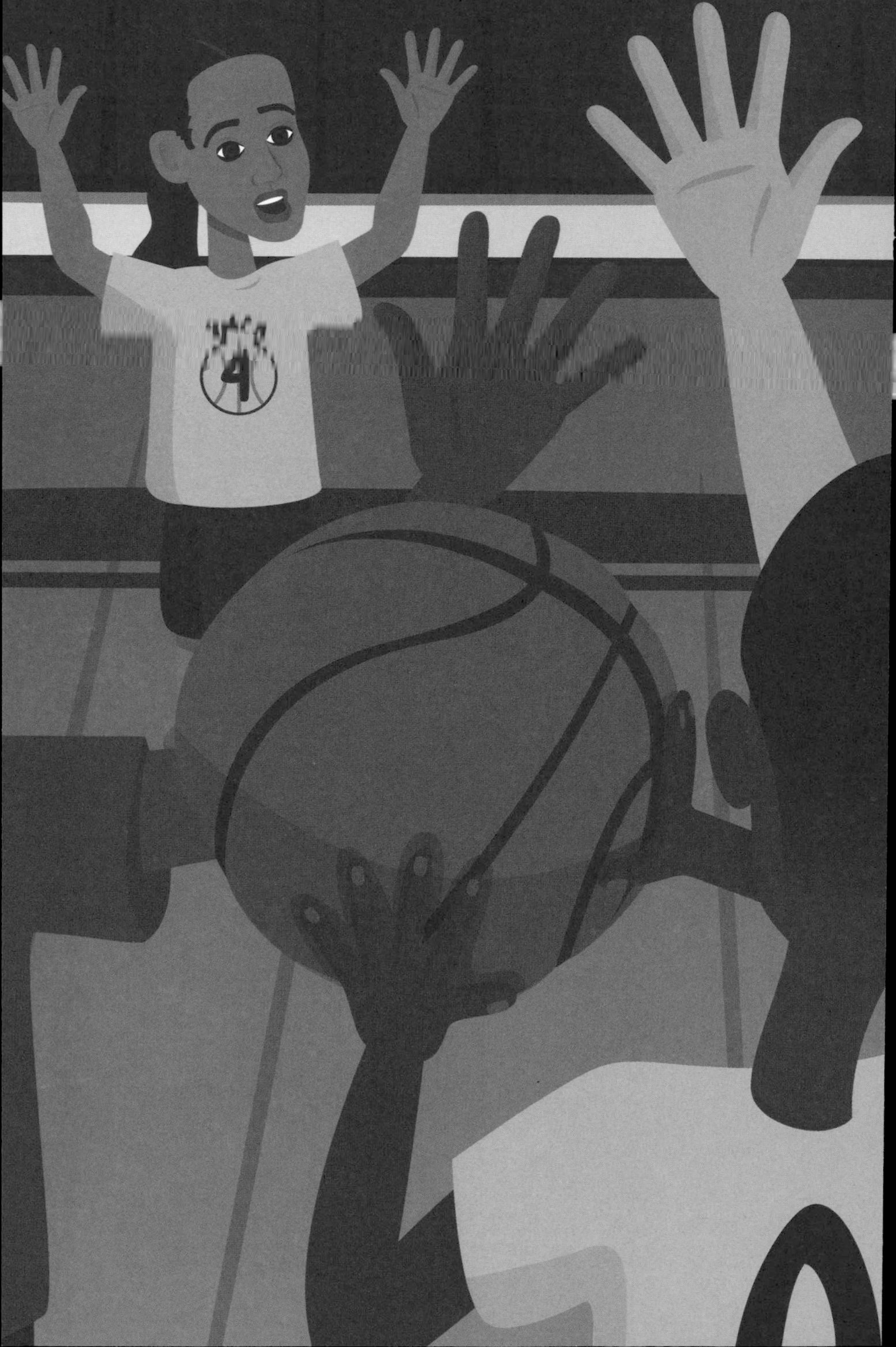
4

Chapter 6

Skylar Plays Basketball at the Y

Mom wants to keep Skylar away from the physical sports… but Daddy isn't helping. He and Skylar always play on the adjustable basketball hoop he gave Skylar when she turned three.

The games are serious.

Daddy and Skylar are Team Diggins, and they always face the same duo, Detlef Schrempf and Drazen Petrovic. The other team is not American, and they are great shooters.

The games are chaotic.

Daddy and Skylar play for Team Diggins *and* Team Schrempf-Petrovic. Daddy is also the announcer:

"Petrovic for three, and it's good!
Team Diggins trail by three.
They need a basket.
[illegible]
It's good! The crowd is going wild!"

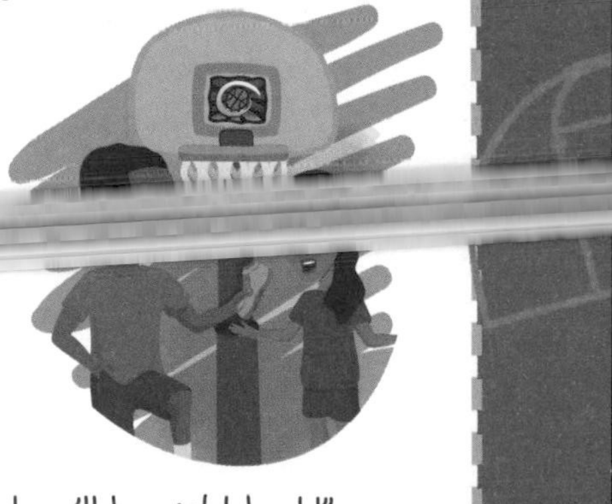

The games even have commercials.

"There's a timeout on the floor, and we'll be right back!"

Daddy recites popular ads like for Frosted Cheerios and Power Wheels. Skylar usually smiles and laughs. But sometimes she stews because she missed a few shots in a row before the break.

At halftime, Daddy interviews Skylar.

"You guys are playing well. What do you need to do to win this game?" he asks.

"We need to get more rebounds!" Skylar declares.

The games go down to the wire.

And Skylar always makes the last shot.

As the clock operator, Daddy also makes sure the time never runs out. He'll get an extra rebound or two and ensure Skylar drills the game-winner.

"It's good! Team Diggins wins! The crowd is going crazy!"

Skylar does not tire of the games, or the cheers, even if they are not real.

Yet.

At six, Skylar is ready to show what the youngest star of Team Diggins can do!

She plays *co-ed* basketball at the YMCA. Co-ed means that boys and girls play together.

On her team, there are nine players, and she is the only girl.

In her first game, Skylar quickly realizes something: the boys will not pass her the ball!

Minutes into the game, Sammy gets double-teamed, and Skylar is wide open near the free-throw line.

She waves her hands and says, "I'm open, I'm open!"

Sammy keeps dribbling and gets off a shot, which he misses.

On the next possession, Tony dribbles the ball up the court, and Skylar sprints past everyone else. She has a straight path to the basket for a layup.

Tony passes it to Sammy.

The game ends, and Skylar's team loses, 12-4.

Skylar does not receive a single pass. She does not shoot the ball once.

Afterwards, she stomps off the court and heads straight for the locker room. Mom is not far behind.

"That's not fair!" Skylar tells her mom. "I can dribble, I can score. Why won't they give me a chance?"

Mom knows the *real* answer, but she encourages Skylar.

"Just be patient," Mom says. "In time, they'll see your talent."

Before the second game, Daddy tells the team that it is important to let everyone handle the ball on offense.

"Try to make sure everyone touches the ball before we shoot," he says.

But after five minutes, Skylar still does not get the ball.

Skylar's team trails 6–0.

Then Sammy dribbles the ball off his foot and it bounces right into Skylar's hands. Without hesitation, Skylar dribbles and drives toward the basket, and she puts up a left-handed layup. She scores!

She has a dozen family members watching on the sideline, and they all stand up and cheer. She *loves* the applause.

Sammy and Tony share cunnin~~~~

The opposing team misses a layup, and Tony passes Skylar the ball. She drives; she scores.

On the next possession, Skylar drives and scores again.

When the referee whistles the game over, Skylar's team wins 8–6.

Skylar scores all eight points.

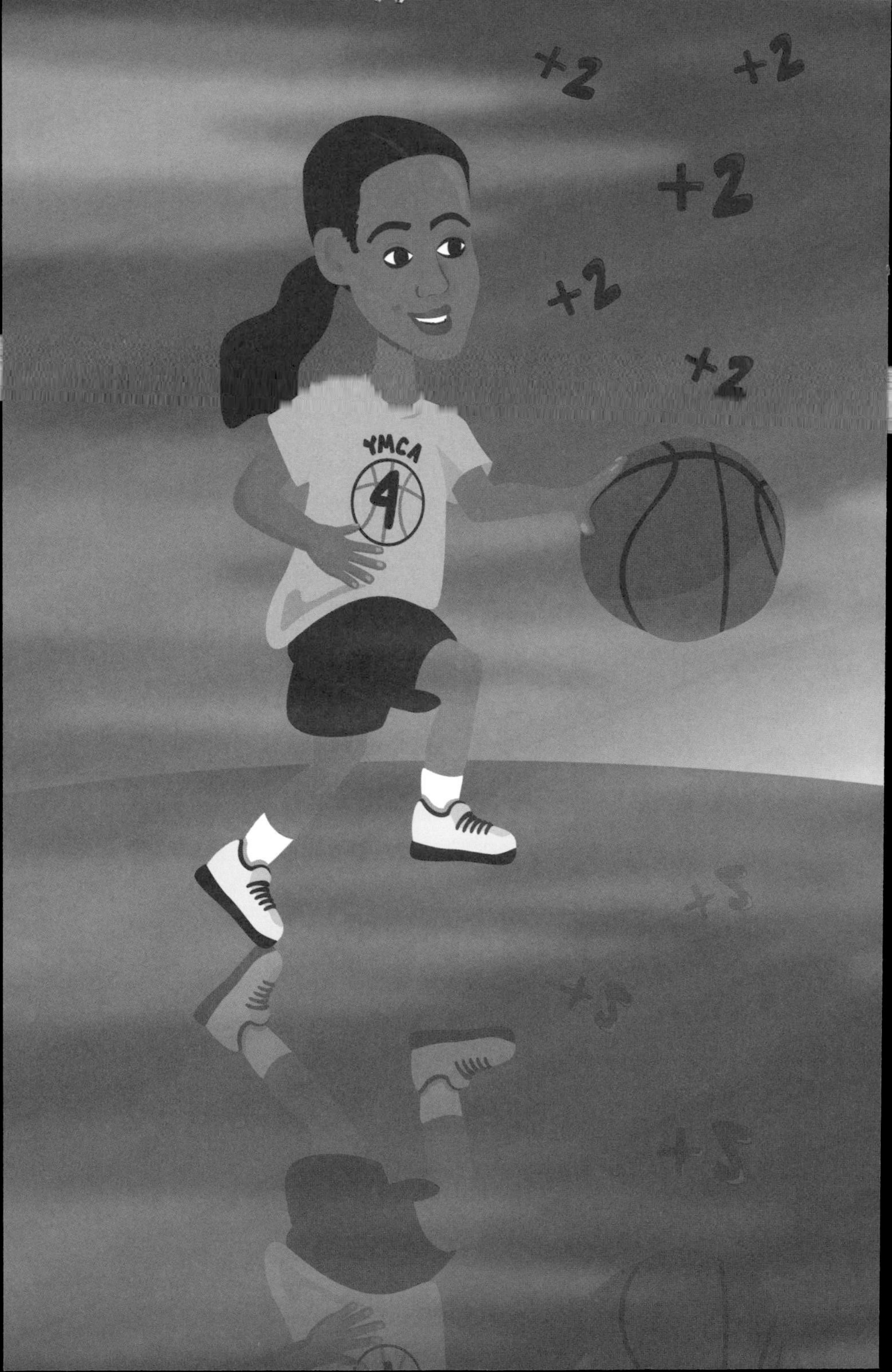
+2
+2
+2
+2
+2
YMCA
4

There is No "i" in Team

Skylar is her team's best player. She hustles, she rebounds, and she scores almost all the points. After a few wins, other parents look at Daddy funny.

Daddy frequently reminds Skylar to pass to her teammates.

"He's open, he's open!" Daddy says.

Skylar dribbles, drives to the basket, and scores another layup.

Skylar steals a pass at midcourt, and she darts toward the basket again.

"Pass to Ricky!" Daddy says.

Skylar does not want to pass to Ricky because he struggles to catch the ball, and

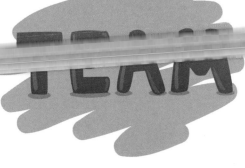

... she thinks back to their first game, when the boys would not pass to her. They did not think she could play. They were wrong, she was right.

Skylar does as Daddy says... and Ricky drops the ball out of bounds.

Skylar turns toward her Daddy, sticks out her hip, and raises her arms to the side, palms up, and yells, "See!"

Skylar's team is losing, and she is mad. With three minutes left in the game, Tommy passes Ricky the ball, and he starts to dribble toward the hoop.

Skylar does not believe Ricky can score. So as Ricky jumps toward the basket, Skylar jumps higher, slams into her teammate, and swats the ball out of bounds. If they were opponents, the official would call a foul.

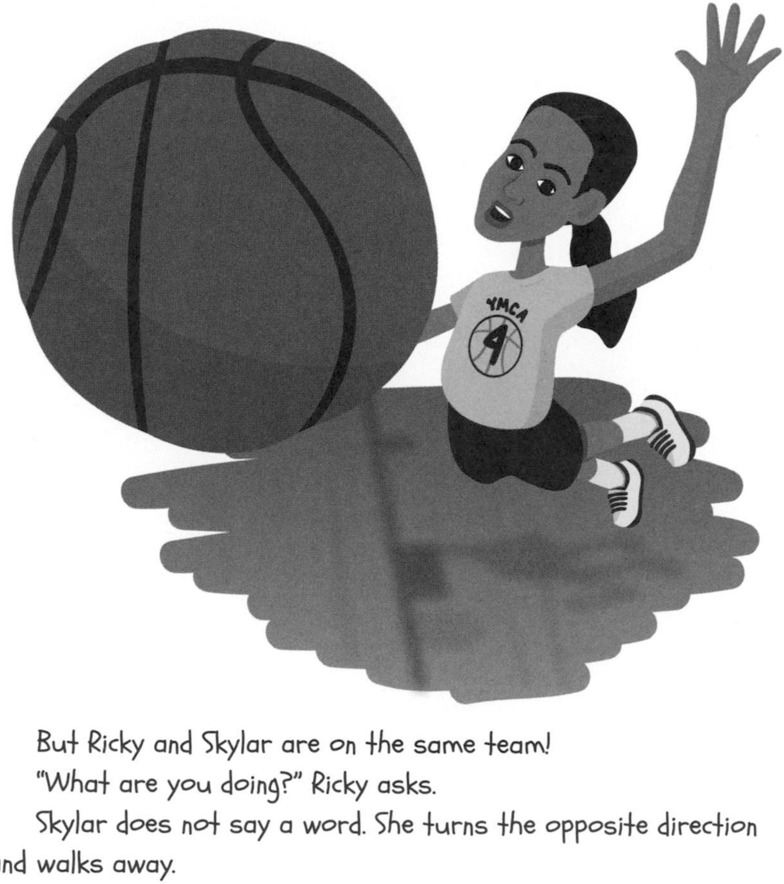
YMCA
4

But Ricky and Skylar are on the same team!

"What are you doing?" Ricky asks.

Skylar does not say a word. She turns the opposite direction and walks away.

After the game, Daddy pulls Skylar aside.

"You lose the ball sometimes too," Daddy tells Skylar.

As her lip quivers, Skylar loudly says, "But Ricky misses all the time!"

Daddy takes a deep breath.

Daddy's Rule

"You have to make your teammates better," Daddy says. "Our team is only as good as our weakest link."

Players and parents clear the court, but Skylar sits on the bench alone. She feels bad, but she is still upset. She likes to win, but she *hates* to lose.

Skylar *knows* she can score more often than Ricky, or Sammy, or anyone else on her team. Daddy, though, could be onto something.

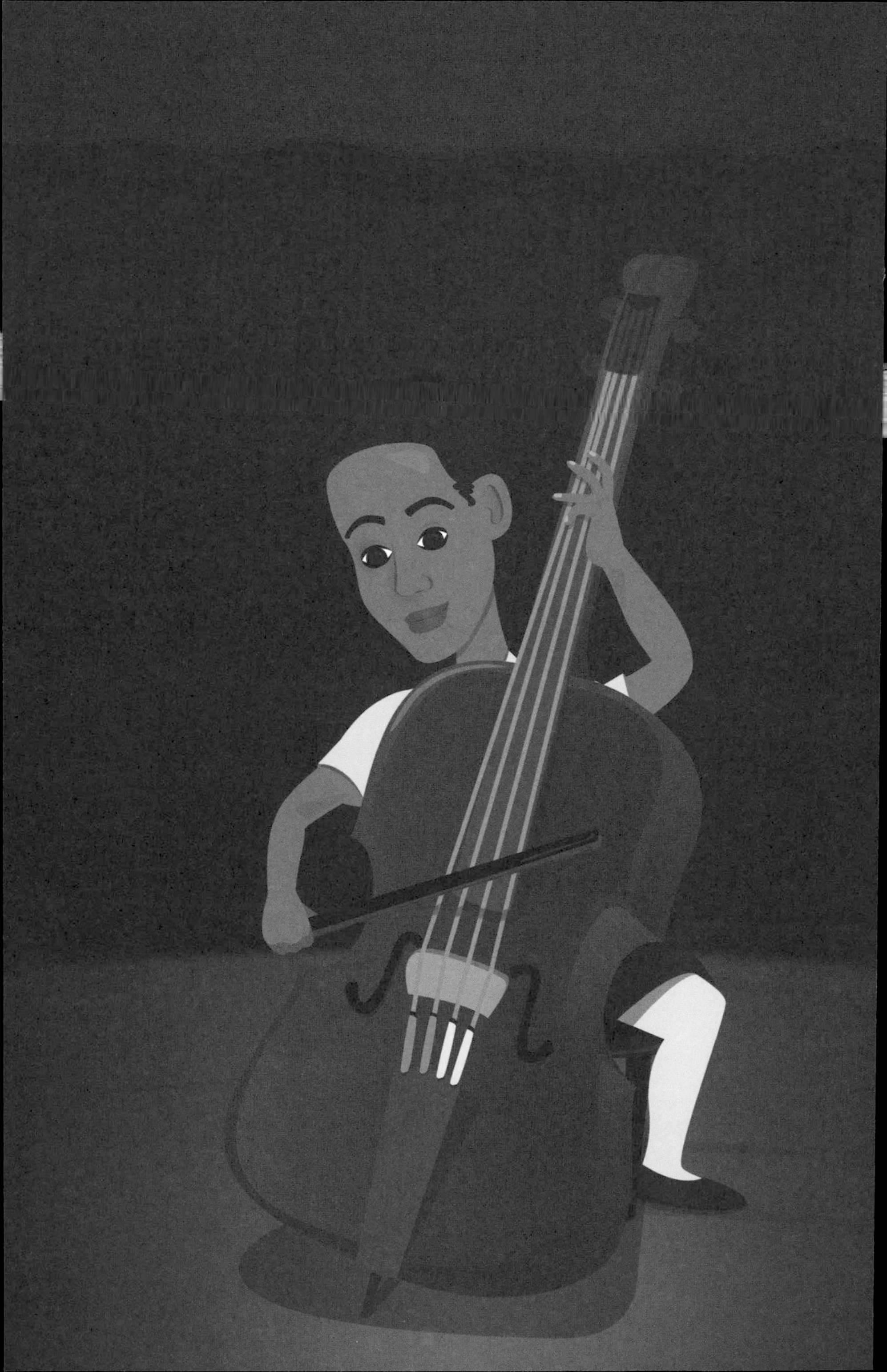

Chapter 8
Hungry for School

Skylar loves Wilson Elementary School. First, the school is close to Granny Stella's. Second, the school is so much fun! She plays on the jungle gym, she participates in basketball and football with the boys, and she leads her peers.

"Let's do this," Skylar tells her classmates one day, running them through an obstacle course.

"Let's do that," Skylar says on another day, pointing to the basketball court.

Mrs. Keyes, a playground monitor, admires how Skylar takes charge but does not abuse her influence. When they play a sport, Skylar tries to create fair teams, but often makes the opposing team better than her own. And when someone struggles, Skylar lifts them up rather than breaking them down.

_____ because Mrs. Keyes is very different from other teachers.

Right away, Mrs. Keyes teaches a week-long lesson on bears. Skylar loves it! The students read assorted books about bears and discover the different characteristics and types from around the world. Mrs. Keyes even has a stuffed mascot named "Gary the Grizzly." Each day, a student takes Gary home and writes about his visit to their house.

Skylar documents how Gary sits at the table for taco night

and participates in one of her epic mini-hoop games with Daddy. Daddy pretends to be Indiana Pacers forward Detlef Schrempf.

Gary blocks Detlef's shot, Skylar writes. *Then Skylar grabs the rebound, dribbles down the court, and shoots a three-pointer from the top of the key.*

It's good! Skylar and Gary win! Skylar and Gary win!

Skylar asks Daddy to take a picture of her with Gary in front of the hoop.

Some teachers make sure everyone understands a lesson before anyone can move on. But others allow each student to learn at his or her own pace. Mrs. Keyes embraces this philosophy. She constantly challenges and stretches the limits of every student.

Mrs. Keyes recognizes that Skylar and three other classmates are very smart and hungry for more difficult work. In math, they practice multiplication and division while other students practice subtraction and word problems. In English, they read books written for fourth graders.

Then Mrs. Keyes has a thought: *can these students read and understand Charlotte's Web?*

The book is a classic. It tells the story of a pig named Wilbur and his unlikely friendship with a spider named Charlotte. The plot of *Charlotte's Web* is complex and intricate, like a spider's web.

Can Skylar and her classmates keep up?

There is celebration of friendship and life, but there is also death and injustice.

Can Skylar and her classmates handle the material?

They ace Mrs. Keyes' test!

But Mrs. Keyes has one problem with Skylar: she talks too much.

Sometimes Skylar wants to help someone else, or she knows the answer and really, really wants to tell the class. Mrs. Keyes does not appreciate having to correct Skylar so much.

Mrs. Keyes' Rule

"All right," Mrs. Keyes would often say. "What do we need to do? We need to stay focused."

Many times, Mrs. Keyes looks directly at Skylar. Skylar does not talk back, and she always receives Mrs. Keyes warning well.

At Wilson Elementary, Skylar's teachers encourage her to try new things. But in fourth grade, Mom thinks Skylar may have gone overboard.

Skylar plays the violin, and practices and practices for the

...... to play the cello instead. She likes the deeper sound of the cello, and her long fingers feel more natural shifting on a cello than a violin.

"But you've never played the cello," Mom says.

"I think I can do it," Skylar coolly replies.

Mrs. Barnes thinks Skylar can too. The music teacher senses that Skylar has an advanced grasp of music. But even a natural gift requires a lot of hard work.

When she gets home, Skylar usually practices the violin for an hour after dinner. But she ramps up her practice sessions when she switches to the cello four days before the concert. She practices for two hours *before* dinner and one hour *after* dinner.

The concert takes place on a Thursday evening. The auditorium is packed with people. Skylar has 25 relatives in attendance. Some of the students are nervous, but Skylar is not.

Just like in basketball, Skylar revels in the pressure, in the spotlight.

She confidently takes her place, sitting in a wooden chair, with the cello between her legs.

She takes a deep breath.

Mrs. Barnes signals, and everyone begins to play.

Skylar plucks the strings with ease, the deep, powerful sound resonating through the auditorium. She gets in a groove, tuning out the audience and locking in on each note. When the first song ends, she snaps back to reality, and spots her family in the crowd.

Her mom smiles and claps, tears trickling from her eyes.

Skylar smiles back at her mom, proud that all her extra hard work has paid off. In the classroom, on the court, or in the orchestra, Skylar likes to challenge herself and see the results.

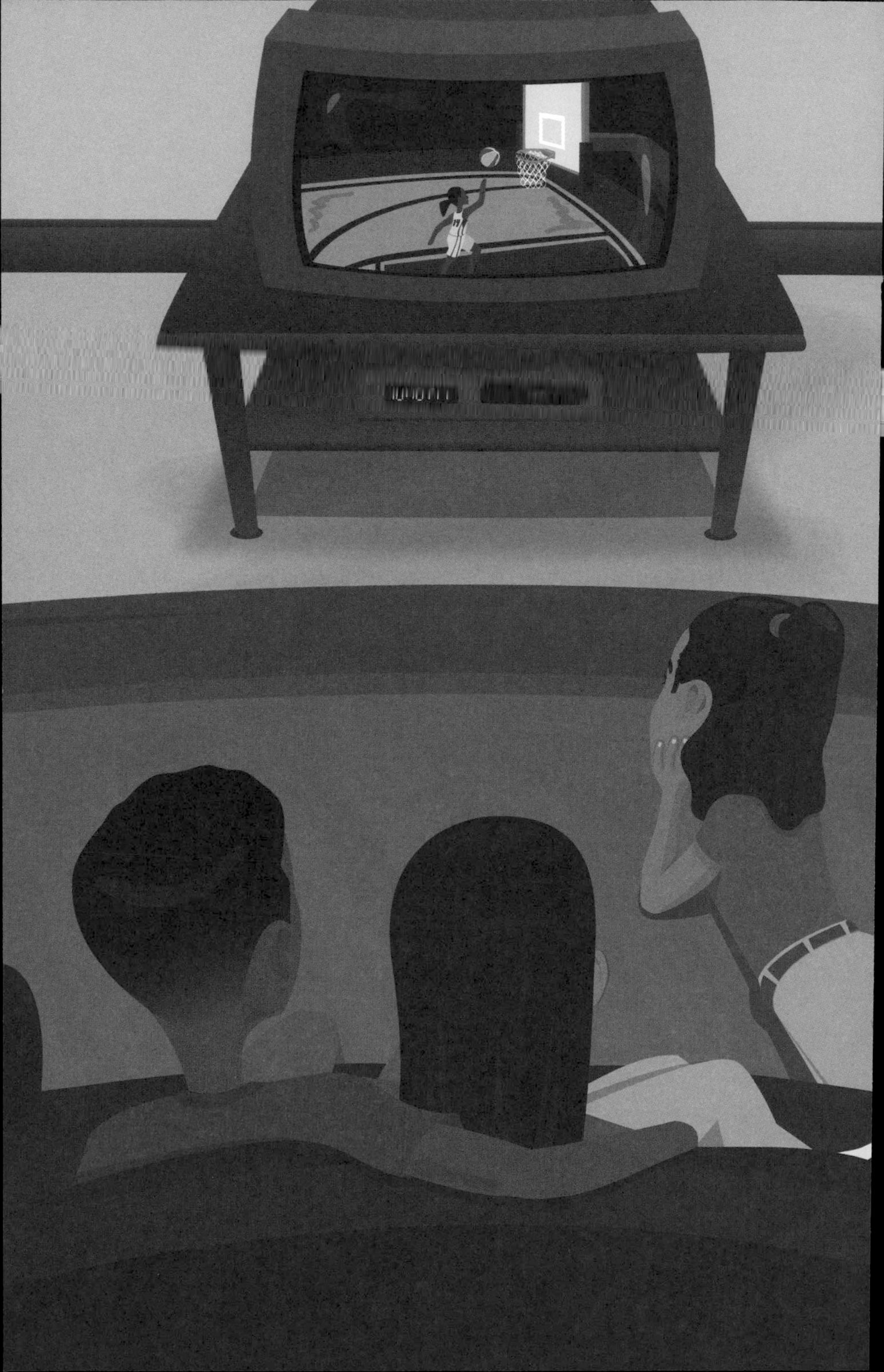

Chapter 9

Seeing Her Future

"Hurry up, Mom!" Skylar shouts. "The game's about to start!"

It's June 21, 1997. Skylar lays down on the floor, in front of the television in the family room, ready to watch the first Women's National Basketball Association (WNBA) game ever.

"Skylar, don't sit too close to the television," Mom says as she takes a seat on the couch next to Daddymoe.

Skylar cannot believe there's a professional basketball league for women.

FLASHBACK

In the summer of 1996, the U.S. women's team—after a string of disappointing finishes in international competitions—dominates at the Olympics in Atlanta. In front of 32,987 f... ...ding world champions.

Months later, the WNBA hires a president, announces eight teams for its first season, and starts a "We Got Next" campaign.

In the spring of 1997, Skylar sometimes wonders, *Is the WNBA really going to happen?*

It seems too good to be true!

The WNBA's first game pits Leslie's Los Angeles Sparks against Rebecca Lobo's New York Liberty.

Leslie is both elegant—she wears lipstick on the court!—*and* dominant. A few years later, Leslie becomes the first to dunk in a WNBA game!

Skylar [illegible] that WNBA players are different sizes and shapes, and have different styles. But they all have one thing in common: a will to compete.

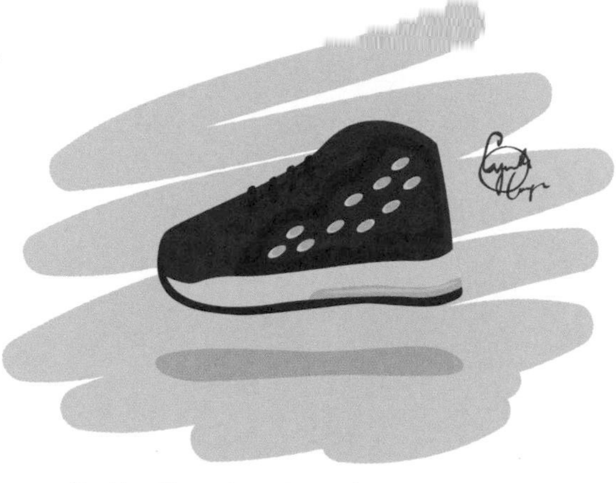

"I'm going to be there one day," Skylar tells her mom.

Mom smiles.

Skylar falls in love that first season with the Houston Comets.

The most famous player on the team is Sheryl Swoopes, one of the stars of the 1996 Olympic team. Skylar also appreciates the surprising star, Cynthia Cooper. Though 34 years old, Cooper plays with joy on the court, slashing to the hoop and celebrating big plays by sticking her elbows out and bending her hands back, with her palms facing up.

"Raise the roof!" Skylar yells, mimicking the move.

Cooper leads the Comets to the WNBA title, also earning both the regular and finals MVP awards.

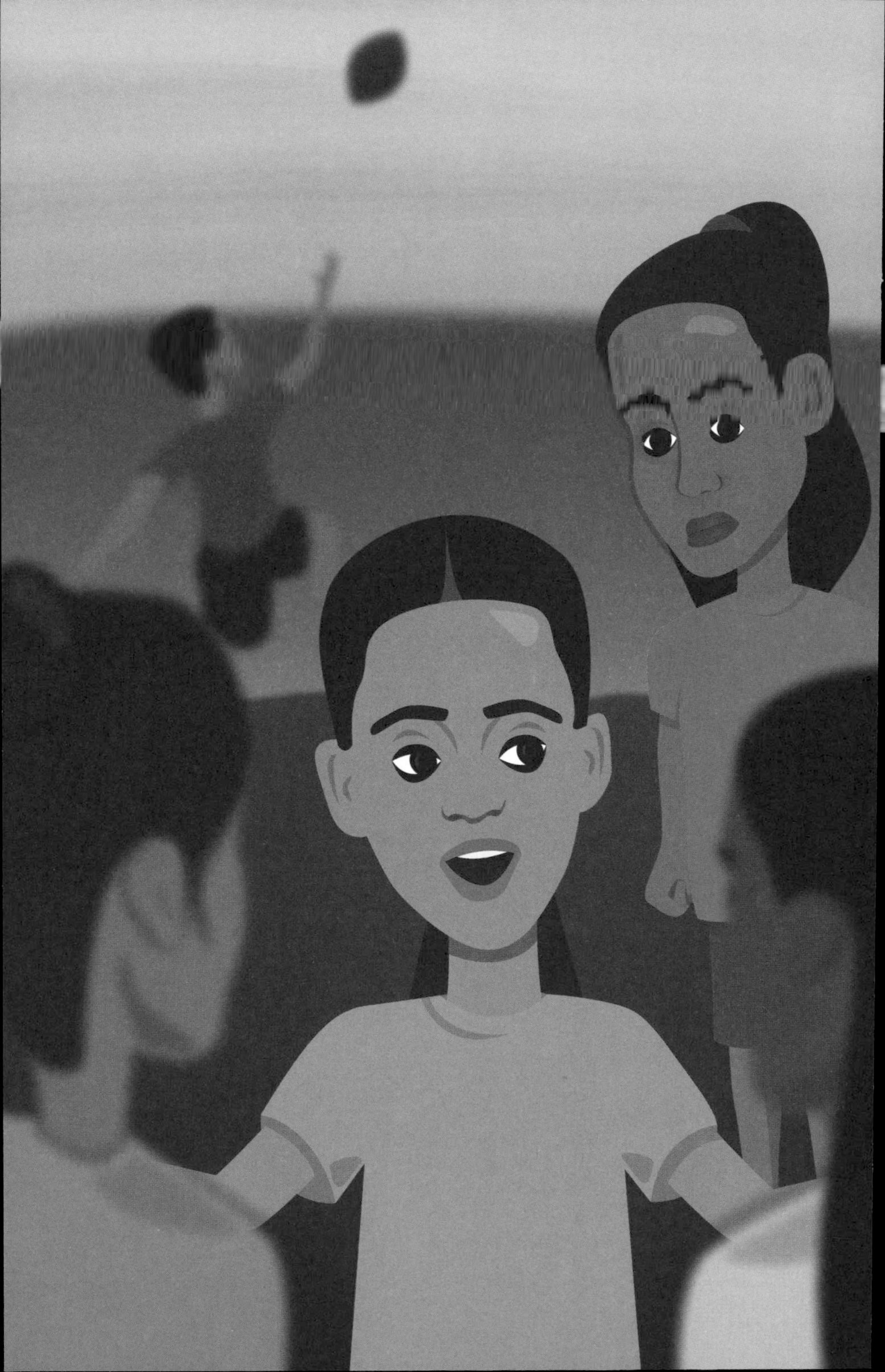

Chapter 10

Keeping Her Cool

Skylar gets ready for school in minutes.

She hops out of bed, briskly walks to the bathroom, brushes her teeth, puts her hair in a ponytail, and heads back to her room to put on her clothes.

Because she plays football and basketball at recess, Skylar does not wear dresses or even jeans. They don't let her bend and run fast enough.

outfit is simple: basketball shorts with a short-sleeved shirt in the spring or summer, and sweat pants with a short- or long-sleeved shirt in the fall and winter.

But Skylar starts to hear mean things from other girls.

"Look at he-she," one whispers as Skylar walks down the hallway.

"Look at all that dirt on her pants," another says loudly. "Ewww!"

These comments make Skylar sad.

She doesn't understand why other girls care what games she plays on the playground or what clothes she wears. One girl is the most persistent in talking trash about Skylar. Her name is Beth, and she's also a fourth-grader.

Unlike Skylar, Beth wears bright-colored dresses and always styles her hair. She does not play—or like—sports, and she spends her weekends competing in beauty pageants. Sometimes, Beth shows up to school with makeup on her face.

Between classes, Skylar heads to the bathroom.

"The boys' bathroom is over there," Beth says, pointing down the hallway.

Skylar grits her teeth and storms past Beth into the girls' bathroom.

The next day, after recess on the playground, the students line up to walk back into the school.

"Hey Skylar," Beth says in front of her friends. "Can I ask you something?"

"What?" Skylar suspiciously responds.

"Why are you such a tomboy?" Beth asks.

Skylar is not offended, but some people think *tomboy* is an unkind term for girls based on stereotypes of boys. Skylar has heard others whisper that about her before, but Beth brings it up in front of a lot of classmates.

Skylar does not respond. She is embarrassed.

Beth isn't done with her questions.

"What's wrong with you?" she demands.

Just then, the bell rings. Mrs. Moore swings a door open and waves the children inside. Beth and her friends laugh as they walk away.

At home, Skylar trembles with anger.

"What's wrong, Skylar?" Mom asks.

Skylar is always honest with her mom, and she does not like to keep secrets from her. But she wonders if she will get in trouble if she tells her mom what's *really* on her mind.

Skylar decides to find out. She tells her mom all about Beth, finishing with what happened after recess.

"Can I hit her in the throat one time so she stops talking?" Skylar asks.

"Absolutely not," Mom replies. "Beth won't be the first person to say something mean to you, and she certainly won't be the last. In fact, you'll probably hear much worse as you get older.

"You know that . . . . take the high road.

Skylar persists.

"Why do *I* always have to take the high road?" Skylar shouts. "Mom, please let me beat this girl up. I know I could."

Mom walks closer to Skylar and puts her arm around her.

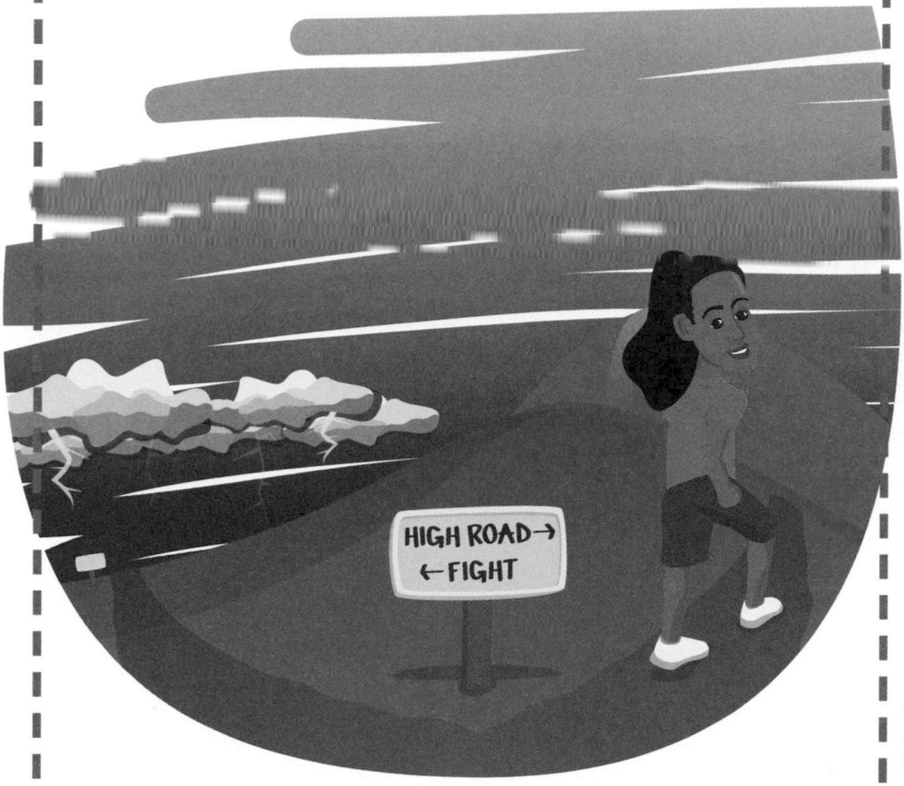
HIGH ROAD→
←FIGHT

Mom's Rule

"Don't ever let anyone else have control over your emotions," Mom says. "Don't let anyone turn you into someone you're not."

Skylar feels better because she loves her mother, and she has vented about her frustrating day at school. And though she doesn't fully understand everything, Skylar obeys her mom and does not punch or even confront Beth.

Skylar does something that Beth does not like. Skylar *ignores* her.

For a few days, Beth makes rude comment. But Skylar never reacts, and Beth eventually gives up.

Skylar is glad she listened to her mom.

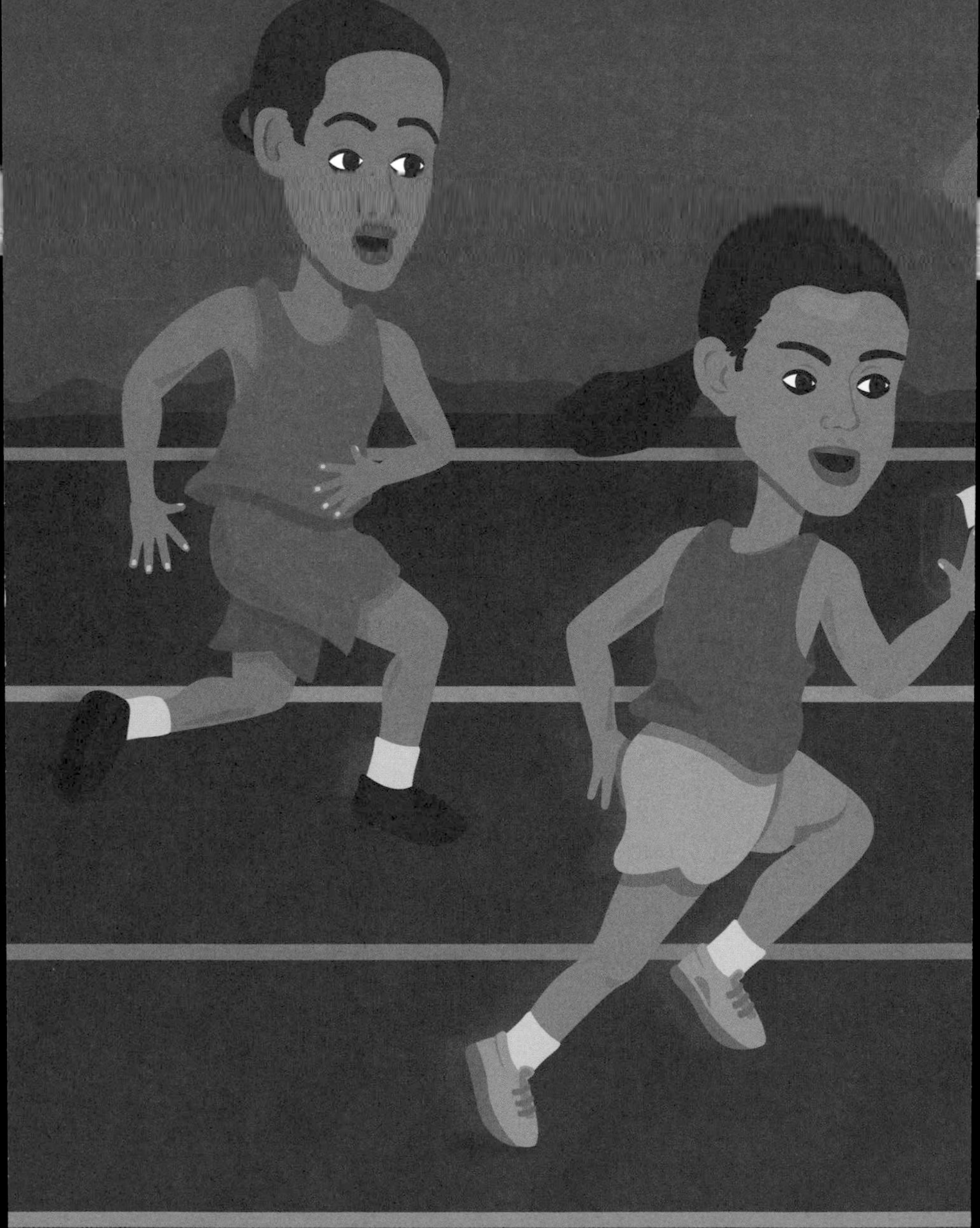

Chapter 11

Losing the Race

In fifth grade, Skylar loves basketball. She still plays football with the boys on the playground at school and in yards with cousins and neighbors.

Mom, though, insists Skylar at least try other sports.

"Skylar, I signed you up for track."

Skylar knows better to protest or whine. She also knows not to ignore her mother.

"All right, Mom," Skylar responds, forcing a smile on her face. "Thank you."

Coach Mills tests Skylar and her track teammates. He makes them run races of different lengths and practice different field events, like shot put and high jump.

Skylar feels fast.

Because she plays basketball, Skylar ~~~~~~~~~~~~~~ to blow past defenders ~~~~~~~~~~~~~~. She runs a lot on the court, she never has to continuously run for minutes without a break.

The day before Wilson Elementary School takes part in a track meet, Coach Mills informs his athletes which events they'll participate.

"Skylar, you're going to run the 400," Coach Mills says. "Nancy, you're going to..."

Skylar looks up. Coach surprised her. She figured she'd run the 100– or 200–meter sprints. Those are short races, just around a part of the track. The 400 is a full lap!

Skylar thinks her strength is her speed, not her endurance. At home, she explains her concern to her mom.

"Coach put me in the 400," Skylar says, "and I don't know why."

Skylar does not get much empathy from her mom.

"He put you there because he believes you can do it," Mom says. "He picked you for a reason, so try it."

At the meet, there are elementary school athletes from four different schools. As she warms up for the 400, Skylar hears from the girl in the next lane.

"Hi, I'm Emily. What's your name?"

Skylar is nervous.

"I'm Skylar, and I'm going to win this race," she blurts out. "I'm so fast I could run backwards and still beat you! I'm so fast I could run in high heels and still win!"

Emily juts her head backward and scrunches her eyebrows.

"Who is she talking to?" Emily asks another competitor.

The six racers line up, and the horns sounds.

Skylar jumps out to an early lead. She knows not to run her fastest in the beginning of the race or else she will run out of energy too early. But she still shows off her speed, building a comfortable lead.

As she completes the first stretch, Skylar realizes two things: she's still has a long way to go, and she's tiring quickly!

Emily gets closer and closer, and then she breezes past Skylar.

Wait until I get my second wind, Skylar thinks. *I can still win this race!*

Emily builds a bigger and bigger lead... and Skylar loses more and more ground to other runners. Her lungs are burning because she does not usually run this far.

When she crosses the finish line, she doubles over, trying to rest and suck in air. After a few moments, she sees the results.

She finishes last.

Emily wins—by a wide margin.

Skylar freaks out when she returns to the stands near her teammates. She cannot believe the result.

Last place? she thinks. When Skylar competes, she excels and wins.

She does not like swimming, tennis, or gymnastics, but Skylar assumes—with a little practice and hard work—she *could* be great at any of those sports.

Last place? she thinks again.

At home, Skylar expresses her shaken confidence to her mom.

"I know I'm not the strongest, and I'm sure not the tallest," she says. "But I'm also not the fastest? How did I finish last in the race?"

Mom takes a deep breath. She lifts Skylar's chin up, so they can look one another in the eyes.

"Do not worry about how others perform, or what place you finish," Mom says.

Mom's Rule

"You don't have to be the best," Mom says, "but you have to be *your* best."

Later, as she lies in bed, Skylar reflects on her day.

If my size and speed are not going to get me to the WNBA, she thinks, *then what will?*

She does not come up with a good answer before she nods off to sleep.

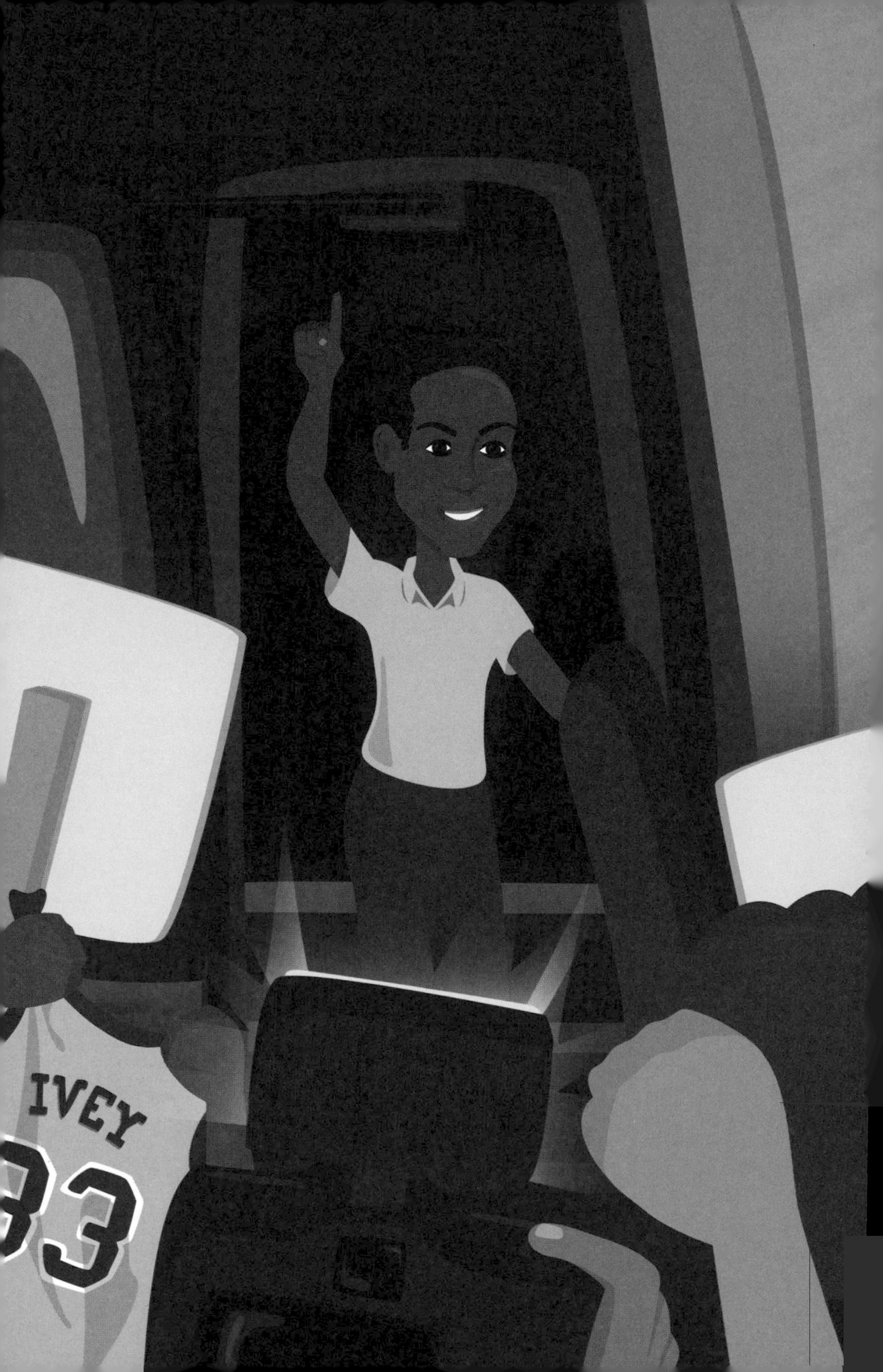
IVEY
33

Chapter 12

Irish Win National Title

As her passion for basketball grows, Skylar pays more and more attention to the Notre Dame women's basketball team. During the 1999–2000 season, the "Fighting Irish" finish with a school-record 27 wins. They reach the NCAA Tournament's "Sweet 16," meaning they were two wins short of playing in the championship game!

Expectations are high for the new season. Ruth Riley is the Fighting Irish's best player. But Skylar cannot relate to her; Riley is 6 feet 5 inches. Skylar isn't tall.

Skylar likes Niele Ivey. She is closer to Ivey's size (5 feet 7 inches), plays her position (point guard), and has a similar playing style. Ivey is tough, having overcome serious injuries in each of her knees. Each game, Ivey averages 11 points, six assists, and three steals, and she communicates the directions of Coach Muffet McGraw.

Skylar thinks she can do all those things: score and distribute the ball on offense, play tenacious defense, and lead her teammates on the court.

In December, Mom takes Skylar to the Joyce Center, home of the Fighting Irish's basketball teams. The Fighting Irish women's team faces Purdue, a college just two hours south of South Bend.

The game is close, but Notre Dame starts to pull away in the final minutes. During a timeout, Skylar soaks in all the excitement: the buzz of the players on the court and the emotion of the fans in the stands.

"I want to play for Notre Dame," Skylar says.

"Oh, okay baby," Mom says.

Skylar knows her mom is just being polite. But Skylar is serious.

The Irish become the No. 1 team in the country, winning its first 23 games before a one-point loss to Rutgers in New Jersey. But the Fighting Irish finish the season strong, qualifying for the NCAA tournament in St. Louis and cruising into the championship game.

Once again, they face Purdue, so it's an all-Indiana final!

The Irish are down as many as 12 points in the first half, and they trail 66–64 with just over a minute remaining.

But Riley scores the game-tying basket in the post, then she grabs the rebound off a missed shot by Purdue, and draws a foul. At the free-throw line, Riley calmly sinks both free throws to give the Irish the lead.

The Irish hold on. They are the national champions!

South Bend rallies to support the victorious team. When their bus arrives after the five-and-a-half hour drive from St. Louis, hundreds of fans are there to welcome and greet them on campus.

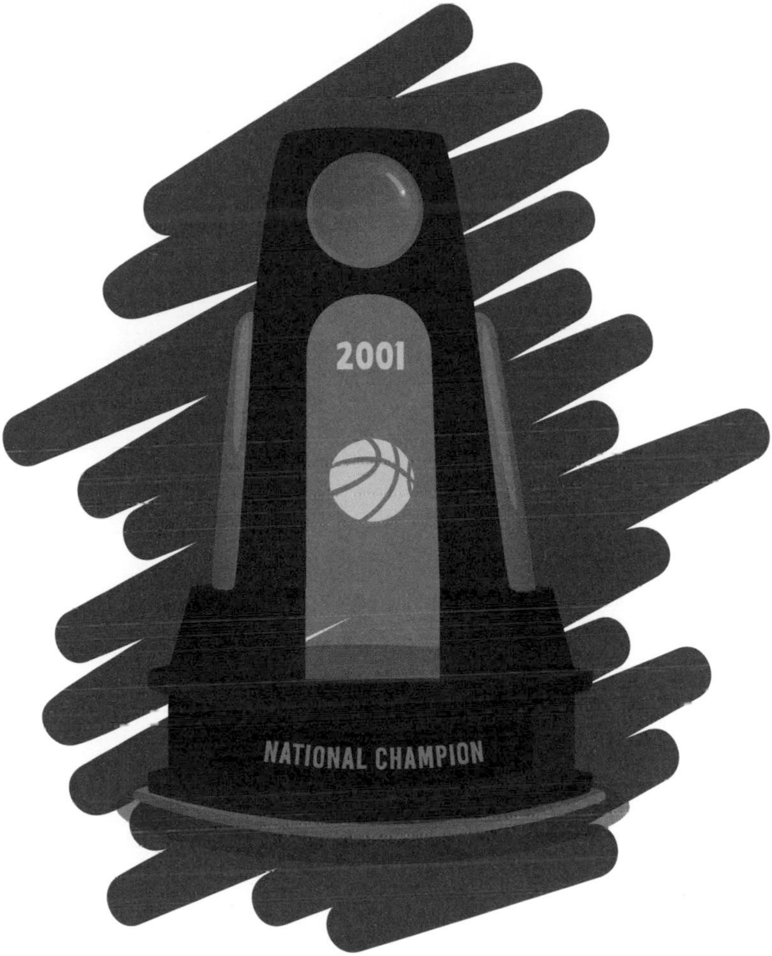
2001
NATIONAL CHAMPION

A celebration is planned, and local schools are invited to send one student to Notre Dame's celebration.

The principal selects Skylar to represent Wilson Elementary!

At the celebration in the Joyce Center, Skylar gets a chance to shake hands and pose in some pictures with the Fighting Irish stars. She's nervous about meeting Niele.

Will she be nice? Will she sign my program?

Skylar feels like she knows Niele from watching her play. *But what if she's different in person?*

When Skylar's moment arrives, Niele is kind and polite. She shakes Skylar's hand, gives her a soft hug, and poses for a picture with her.

Skylar is ecstatic! Now she likes Niele even *more* than before.

As she walks toward the exit later, Skylar looks at her mom, and then looks back toward the court.

"One day, that's going to be me," Skylar says. "I'm going to be up there."

Mom wants Skylar to dream. But Mom knows Skylar is only nine years old. And Notre Dame is one of the top college programs in the entire nation! That's a very big dream.

"Of course you will," Mom says to Skylar, patting her on the head. Skylar doesn't know if Mom believes that, but Skylar sure does.

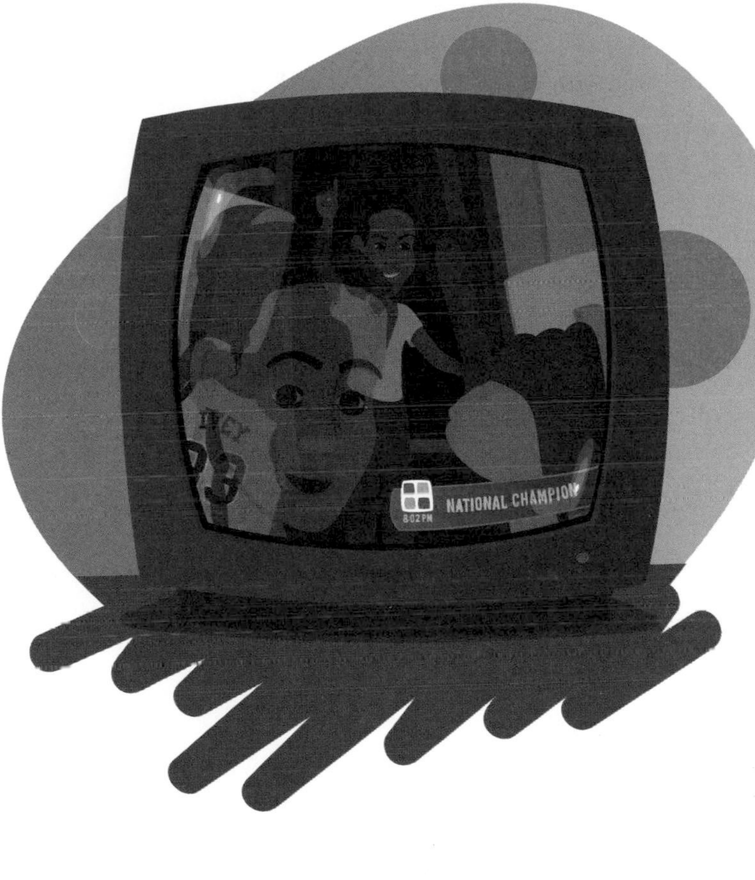
NATIONAL CHAMPION
8:02 PM

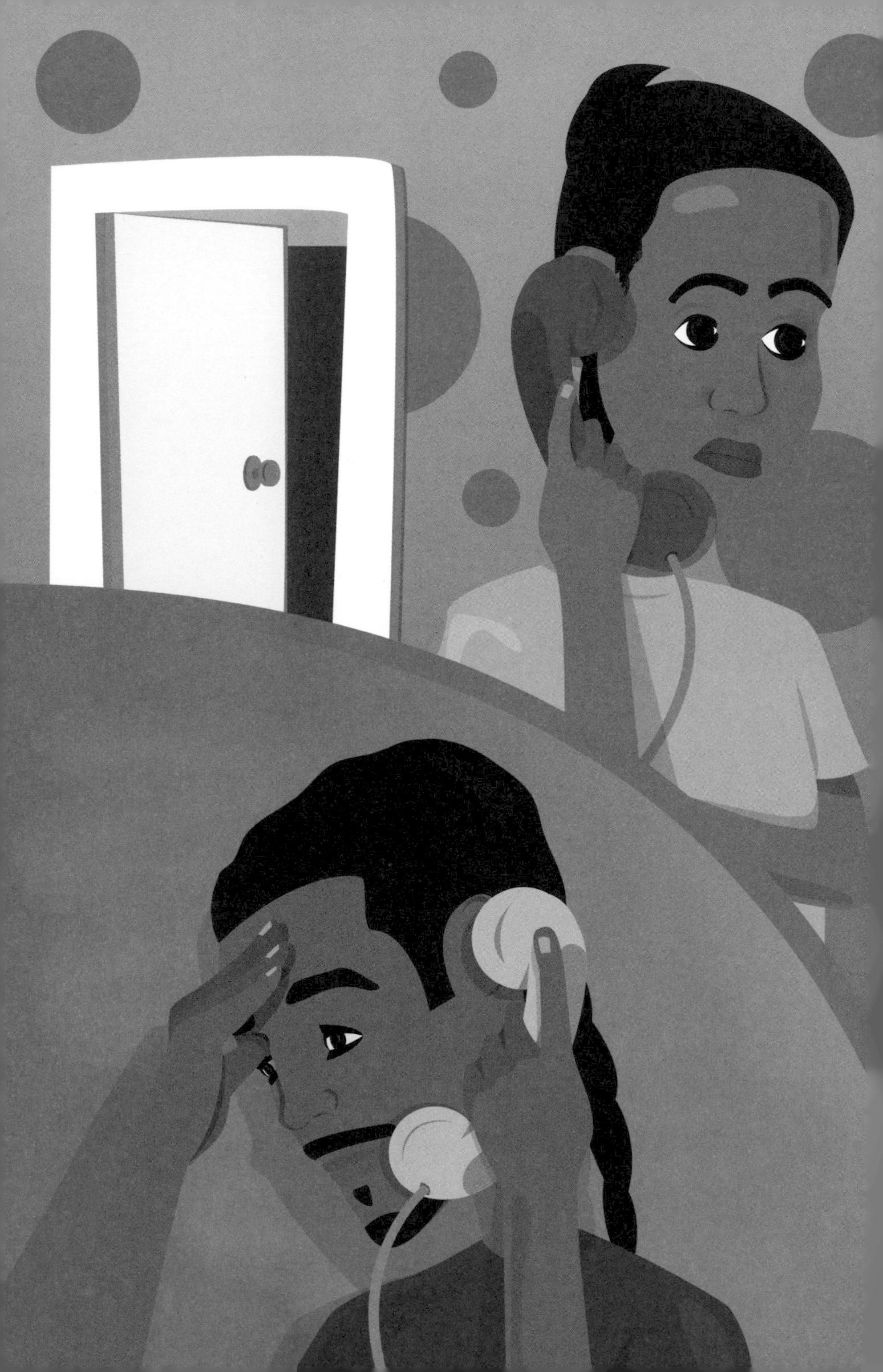

Chapter 13 Heart Broken

At the beginning of fifth grade, Skylar drives home with Mom and sees Daddy's car parked outside. Usually, Mom lets her know when he is coming to visit.

"Why is my Daddy here?" Skylar asks.

There is no answer.

Skylar's eyes connect with Daddy's. He always smiles, but he looks sad now.

"What's wrong, Daddy?" she asks.

Again, no answer.

Skylar, Daddy, and Mom walk into the apartment.

Mom heads to the kitchen, so Skylar and Daddy can sit alone in the living room. Skylar is nervous.

"Daddy, what is it?"

Daddy gently holds Skylar's hands.

"Business has been rough, Skylar," Daddy says quietly. "You know how much I love you, but I have to make a tough decision," Daddy says. "I need to make money painting houses, and I can't do that in South Bend anymore. But I can do it in Florida."

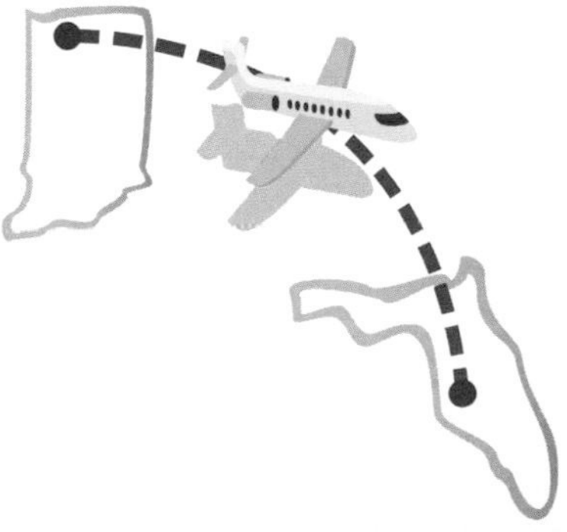

Skylar's lip quivers.

"You mean... you're leaving me?"

"No, no, Skylar," Daddy says.

"It's not like that. But I have to work, and I have to go where the money is. You know Granddad Bennie moved down there, and he said there are a lot of new homes being built."

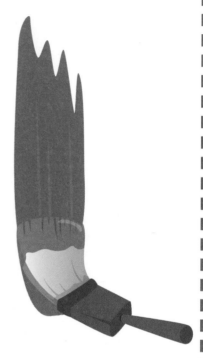

This does not make Skylar feel better. Her chest suddenly hurts.

Is this what a broken heart feels like? she thinks.

"Did I do something wrong?" she asks her Daddy.

Tears well up in Daddy's eyes.

"This is the toughest decision of my life," he says. "But I have to go."

For a few weeks, Skylar is mad at Daddy, so she does not say much when he calls from Florida. She knows this hurts her Daddy's feelings. But she starts to open up more with each conversation, and they speak more frequently.

She does not get to hug him and see him as much, but Skylar still loves her Daddy, and her Daddy still loves her.

Skylar's heart starts to heal.

Daddy flies back to Indiana and visits several times a year. But Skylar's favorite time with him is the weeks she spends with him in Tampa, Florida, each summer. She also gets to hang out with her stepmom Shay and her brothers, Dezz and Tayta. Daddy is silliest—and happiest—when he is with all four of them.

They do everything together, from driving to the beach to

visiting waterparks like Islands of Adventure and theme parks like Busch Gardens.

Daddy really enjoys all the roller coasters, and he later convinces Skylar to ride a new one, Sheikra. That steel coaster goes 70 miles per hour.

Skylar looks up at it. "Wow, that's really high," she says.

"Come on, let's try it!" Daddy says. "Are you afraid?"

Skylar rides many roller coasters but not all of them. This time, though, her competitiveness kicks in. She wants to prove a point to Daddy.

"I'll get on it," Skylar says.

She screams and screams!

She regrets accepting her Daddy's challenge because she does not like rides with big drops. Sheikra, of course, features a 138-foot drop into an underground tunnel!

But Skylar survives.

"Let's go again," Daddy says.

Skylar shakes her head no. She's done with Sheikra!

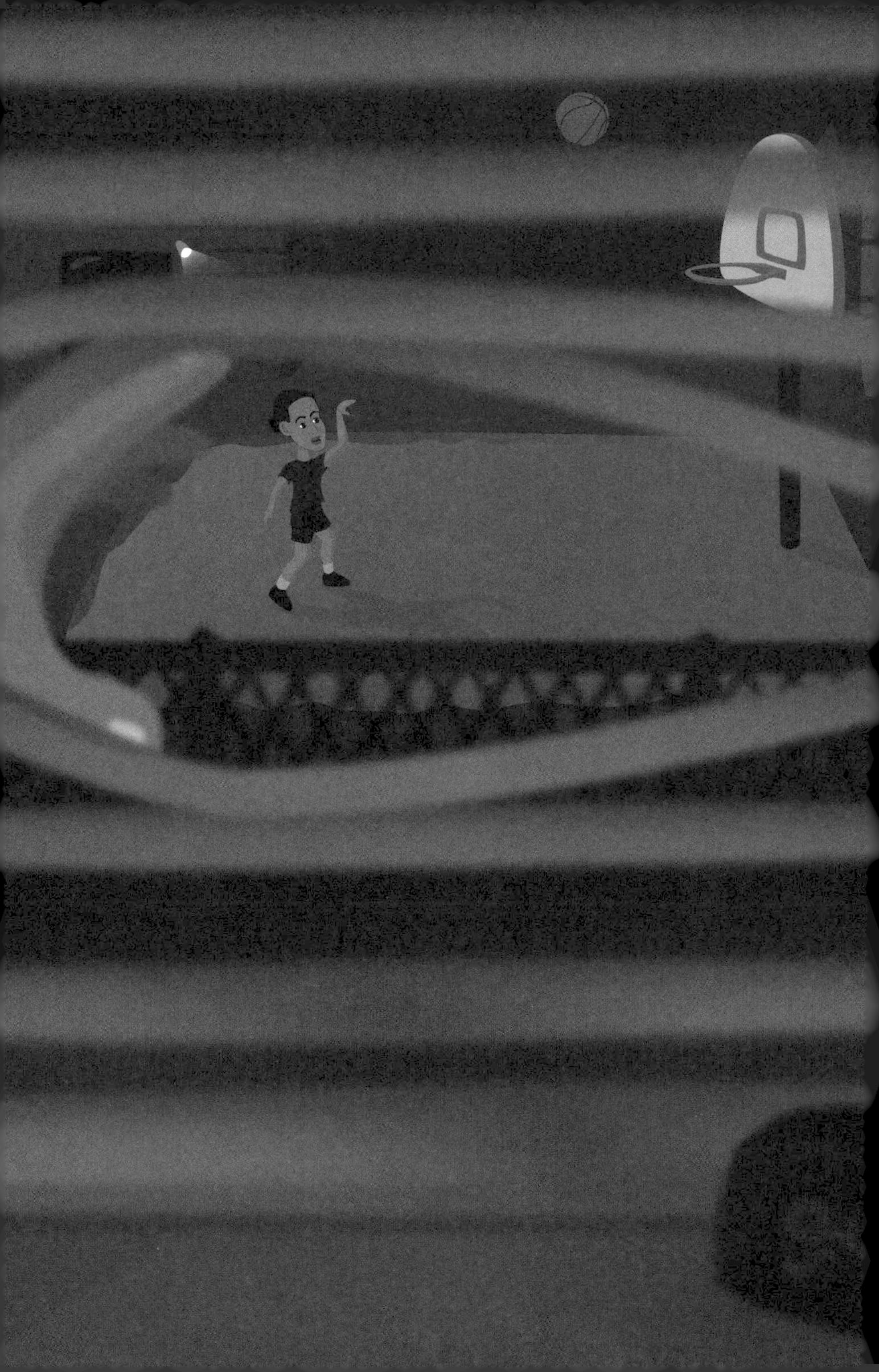

Chapter 14

The Sanctuary

Skylar watches WNBA games on television, and she attends a few games at Notre Dame. But at the King Center, Skylar gets a special treat.

Coquese Washington is one of her favorite Notre Dame players. Coquese plays four years for the Fighting Irish, and she leads them in steals each season and assists three times. Though she earns her undergraduate degree, Coquese decides to also attend Notre Dame's Law School.

To stay sharp, Coquese trains at the King Center. Daddymoe puts her through drills, and Coquese often plays against the men. She is almost always the smallest player on the court, but Coquese does not back down from anyone. She scores a lot of points and dishes out a lot of assists!

Usually, Skylar practices dribbling or shooting on a side basket when adults use the big court. But she sits and intently watches when Coquese plays.

After the pickup games are over, Coquese takes a quick water break then goes through more drills and finishes each workout with free throws.

She must make 10 in a row before she can leave the court.

"See how hard she works, Skylar?" Daddymoe says.

Daddymoe's Rule
"Don't be afraid of having to put the work in to see how good you can become," Daddymoe says. "Practice makes permanent."

Skylar is not afraid of hard work.

After school, Skylar begs her mom to take her to the King Center so she can practice. Daddymoe may be coaching a team, playing in a game, or just managing the facility, but he gives Skylar exercises and drills to work on.

Then, when she gets home, Skylar always heads to her backyard. There's a concrete court with an adjustable rim and clear backboard.

This is Skylar's *sanctuary*, her special place.

She practices on this court constantly. She likes to practice when she is happy, but *especially* when she is mad, sad, nervous, or confused.

Like after her Daddy moves to Florida.

With the glow of the back porch light, Skylar shoots layups, jumpers, and three-pointers for hours and hours.

At 11 p.m. one night, the house phone rings. Calls never come this late at night.

Daddymoe picks up.

"Hello?"

"Is she going to keep shooting that basketball all night long?" neighbor Red asks.

"I'm sorry," Daddymoe says, "But my daughter is working toward her dream. Do you want her to stop?"

Red does not say anything for a moment. "Well, she isn't causing any trouble. I guess the dogs and I will get used to it."

Neighbor Red never complains again.

Skylar works on every facet of her game: footwork for defense, dribbling, running jumpers, three-pointers, and more. With each shooting drill, she challenges herself to see how many she can make in a row before a miss.

Once, she made 50 jumpers from the right elbow of the free throw line!

But no matter what, Skylar always insists on draining at least 100 shots before she leaves her court. Just like Coquese, Skylar wants to push herself when she's tired.

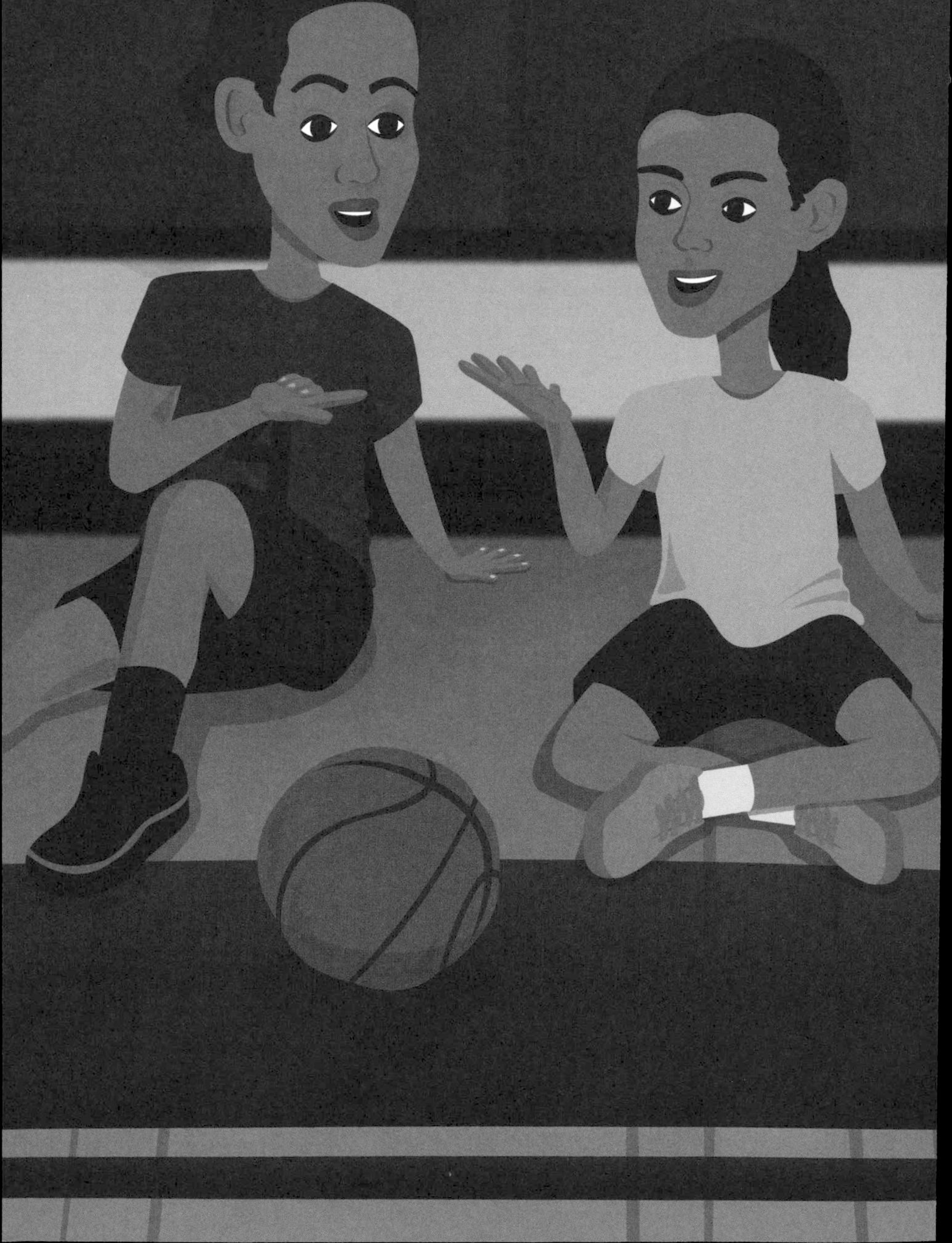

Chapter 15

Connecting with Em

Skylar really likes playing basketball with the boys. The games are fast, and points are plentiful. Not that she has much of a choice—at the King Center, she's the only girl that plays hoops!

As she matures from elementary toward middle school, Skylar basically plays in pickup games every day with the same group of boys. But as time passes, she realizes that the boys are growing bigger, quicker, and stronger at a faster pace than she is.

On a Friday before Columbus Day, Nick brings his cousin Devin to the King Center to play. Devin *looks* like a ball player. He's got the latest Nike sneakers, and matching Jordan shirt and shorts. When he sees Skylar, he whispers something to Nick.

Nick laughs.

On defense, Skylar matches up against Devin. But Devin does not take Skylar seriously. He smiles and makes silly faces. When Skylar gets the ball, Devin mocks her.

"Be careful dribbling that ball,"

he says, "you don't want to break a nail."

Skylar picks the ball up and approaches Devin. She is mad.

"Don't treat me like a girl," Skylar firmly says. "Treat me like a ball player because I don't want any excuses from you after I beat you."

Oooohhhh!

The other boys respect Skylar's response. But Mom starts to get nervous.

The boys pick on her more, and they get more physical with her because they do not want to be embarrassed or outplayed by her. Some resort to aggressive fouls and attempts to block her shot.

"I don't want Skylar to play with boys anymore," Mom tells Daddymoe. "It's unsafe now."

"But there are no girls' teams near us," he reminds her. She doesn't back down.

"I *want* her to play with girls now," Mom firmly says.

"Well, I guess I'll have to create a girls' team," Daddymoe responds.

Daddymoe already runs the Soldiers, a traveling club basketball team for boys. So Daddymoe starts the Lady Soldiers.

He only has one player, Skylar, who is nine years old.

For a few weeks, Daddymoe visits other gyms around South Bend, but he cannot find girls that age who play ball. He looks for 10-year-olds, too. He hands out a flyer to anyone who will take one, inviting them to a tryout for the Lady Soldiers at the King Center.

At a middle school, Daddymoe spots a tall, lanky girl playing well. Sometimes, taller athletes that age are clumsy and trip a lot. But this girl is smooth and quick.

"We need her," Daddymoe tells Skylar. He approaches the tall girl.

"Hi, my name is Maurice," he says.

"Hello, I'm Ashley." she responds.

"I'm starting up a new team called the Lady Soldiers, and I think you should join us." Daddymoe hands Ashley a flyer. Skylar smiles.

"How old are you?"

"I'm 11."

On Saturday, Daddymoe gathers the 17 girls who show up for the Lady Soldiers' tryout.

Ashley is among them.

So is Emily, the one who torched Skylar at the fifth grade track meet. But Emily shows up in blue jean shorts, and her shots not only miss the rim, they miss the backboard altogether.

Maurice instructs the girls to run a simple motion offense but Emily, a point guard, keeps making mistakes. When it's Skylar's turn, she makes everything look so easy. That makes Emily feel worse.

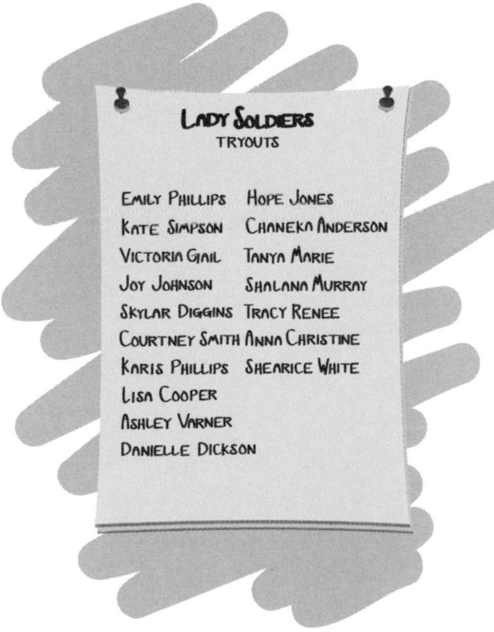

After practice, Emily beelines toward her mother.

"I don't want to do this again," she says.

LADY SOLDIERS
TRYOUTS

EMILY PHILLIPS	HOPE JONES
KATE SIMPSON	CHANEKA ANDERSON
VICTORIA GAIL	TANYA MARIE
JOY JOHNSON	SHALANA MURRAY
SKYLAR DIGGINS	TRACY RENEE
COURTNEY SMITH	ANNA CHRISTINE
KARIS PHILLIPS	SHEARICE WHITE
LISA COOPER	
ASHLEY VARNER	
DANIELLE DICKSON	

On Sunday, though, Emily returns.

"I thought you weren't coming back." Skylar says to Emily.

"My mother made me," she mutters.

Emily struggles to shoot the ball, but her speed is an asset on defense, especially when the team practices the *full-court press*. That's when a team scores a basket then immediately puts pressure on the opponent. Many teams only play defense when the other team crosses half court.

With her endurance and quickness, Emily covers a lot of ground and gets a lot of steals. Daddymoe thinks Emily has a lot of potential.

The Sunday practice lasts two hours, and the girls are exhausted. Most of the players pack up their belongings and stream toward King Center's parking lot. It's almost lunchtime!

Skylar grabs her water bottle from her mom.

"Mom, I don't think Emily likes me," Skylar says. "She probably thinks I was talking trash before that race, but I wasn't being serious."

Mom nods her head.

"Skylar, you know what to do," Mom says.

Mom's Rule

"When you have a problem," Mom says, "talk it out."

Emily sits under a side basket. She sips from her purple water bottle and stretches her legs.

"Can we talk?" Skylar asks Emily.

Emily motions for Skylar to sit by her on the court.

"I was just playing around before that race," Skylar says. "I sometimes make jokes when I'm nervous. Did you know I was kidding?"

"No, I wasn't sure," Emily says. "I didn't really know you that well."

The two of them laugh. For a minute, neither of them speaks.

"I don't have a lot of friends," Skylar quietly confesses. "I don't think a lot of people like me."

Emily crinkles her face.

"Oh my gosh. For real? People are probably just jealous," Emily says, "because you're *really* good at basketball." She pauses.

"I have something to tell you," Emily says to Skylar. "I didn't want to come back today because you're *so* good. I can't dribble like you or shoot like you. I didn't want to look bad."

Skylar appreciates the encouragement.

"Well, you're a really tough defender," Skylar says, "and you're the fastest player on the court. If we practice together, I bet you can improve your game."

Emily and Skylar talk for two hours about their families and their dreams.

A friendship is forged.

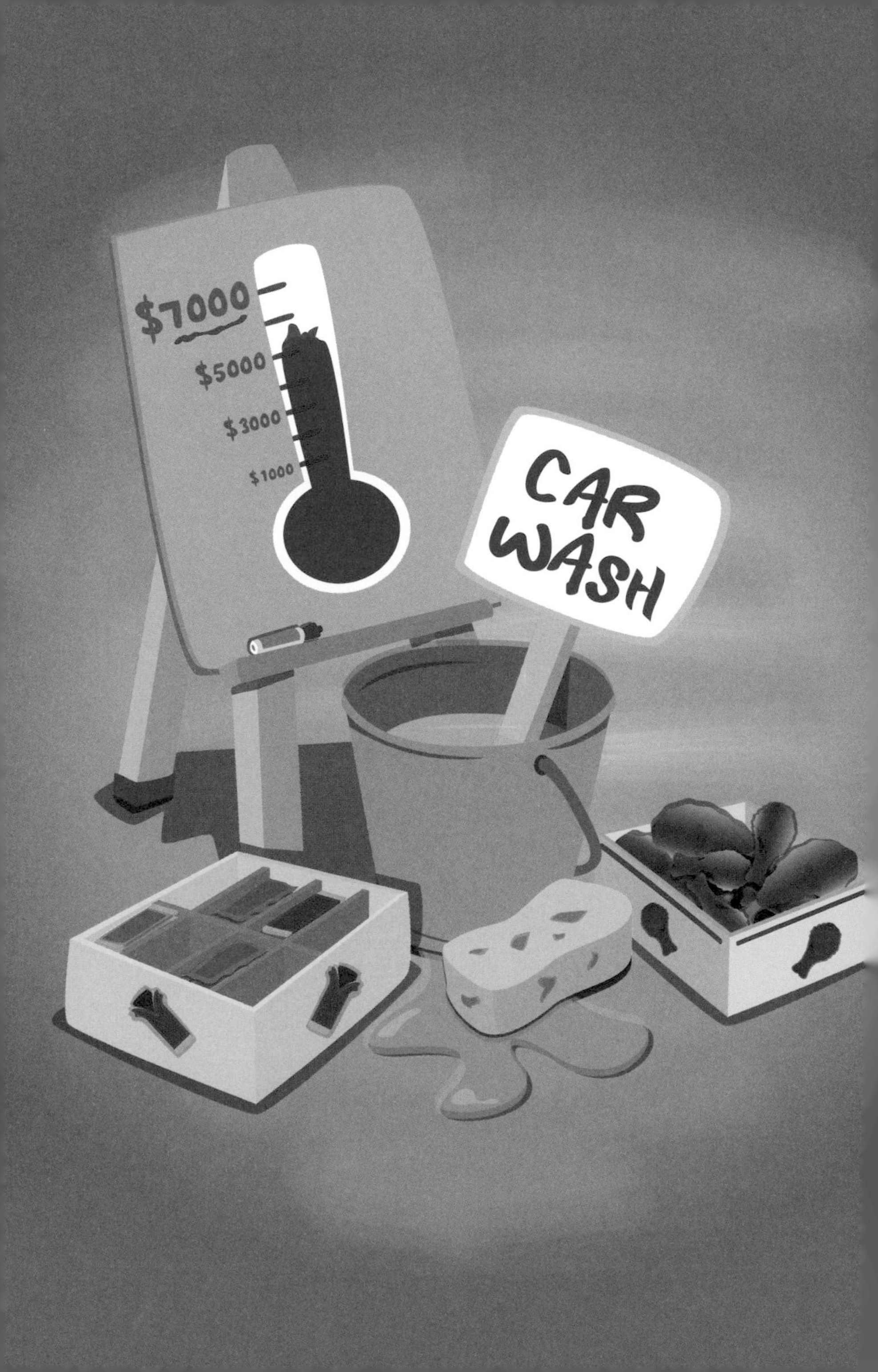
$7000
$5000
$3000
$1000
CAR WASH

Chapter 16

We Are a Family

Daddymoe picks 13 of the 23 players who try out.

Because Ashley and Shalana are 11, the Lady Soldiers must play 11-and-under in the Amateur Athletic Union (AAU).

Skylar will have to play with girls who are two years older!

Will I be able to keep up? she thinks.

At the second practice, Daddymoe arrives with a big brown box.

"What's in there?" Emily asks Skylar.

"I don't know," Skylar responds.

Daddymoe asks the girls to take a knee around him.

"We're not just coming together as a team," Daddymoe says. "We're coming together as a family."

He reaches in the box and pulls out a uniform. One is bright orange with white trim. The other is white with orange trim. The home and away uniforms are sharp. The girls are excited!

Daddymoe turns one of the jerseys around, so the girls can see the back.

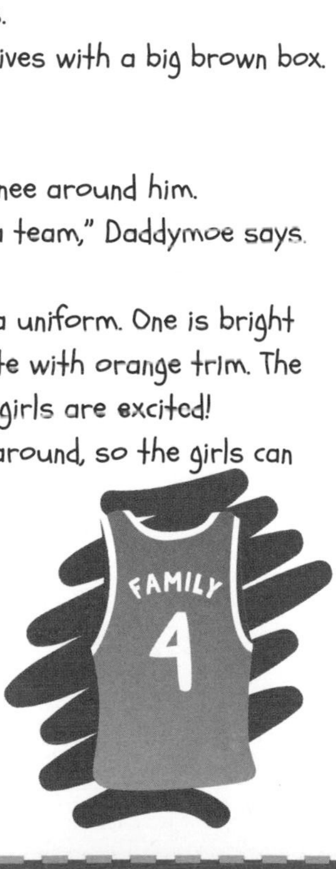
FAMILY
4

There is, of course, a number. But above that—where there is often the player's last name—is a word.

Family.

The girls swarm toward the box and pick their numbers. On the back of every jersey is the word *Family.*

"Always remember," Daddymoe says, "that we are a family."

The Lady Soldiers' first game is at the King Center, and they are all nervous. They bobble balls and miss layups during their warm up because they sneak peeks at the other team.

Before tipoff, the Lady Soldiers circle up.

"All right, Family," Shalana says. "Win on 3."

"1...2...3...Win!"

The Lady Soldiers clobber the other team, 62–25.

A few weeks later, they play in a regional tournament. They finish second. A few weeks after that, they play in the state tournament. They finish fourth. That qualifies them for the AAU National Championships in Tennessee at Austin Peay University.

The school is nearly seven hours away from South Bend.

How will the Lady Soldiers get there?

Some of the girls haven't even been to Chicago, just 90 minutes away!

"Well, we're going to have to raise the money," Daddymoe tells the players.

Assistant coach Steve brings a big, white poster board with

what looks like a thermometer drawn in red and black markers. At the top is $7,000.

"That's how much money we're going to have to raise in order to go to Tennessee," Daddymoe says. "Anyone got that much in their piggybank?"

The girls laugh.

None of the girls lives in a big, fancy house. Many of them only live with their moms.

"We've got two-and-a-half months to raise that money," Daddymoe says, "and we're going to do that as a family."

During the school week, the girls sell candy bars at school and at the King Center. On weekends, the girls wash cars and trucks for $5 each.

Emily is bold, so she does not hesitate to ask customers if the team can keep the change when they get 10- and 20-dollar bills.

By late June, the girls reach their $7,000 goal. They will get to compete in the AAU National Championship.

Can they win it all?

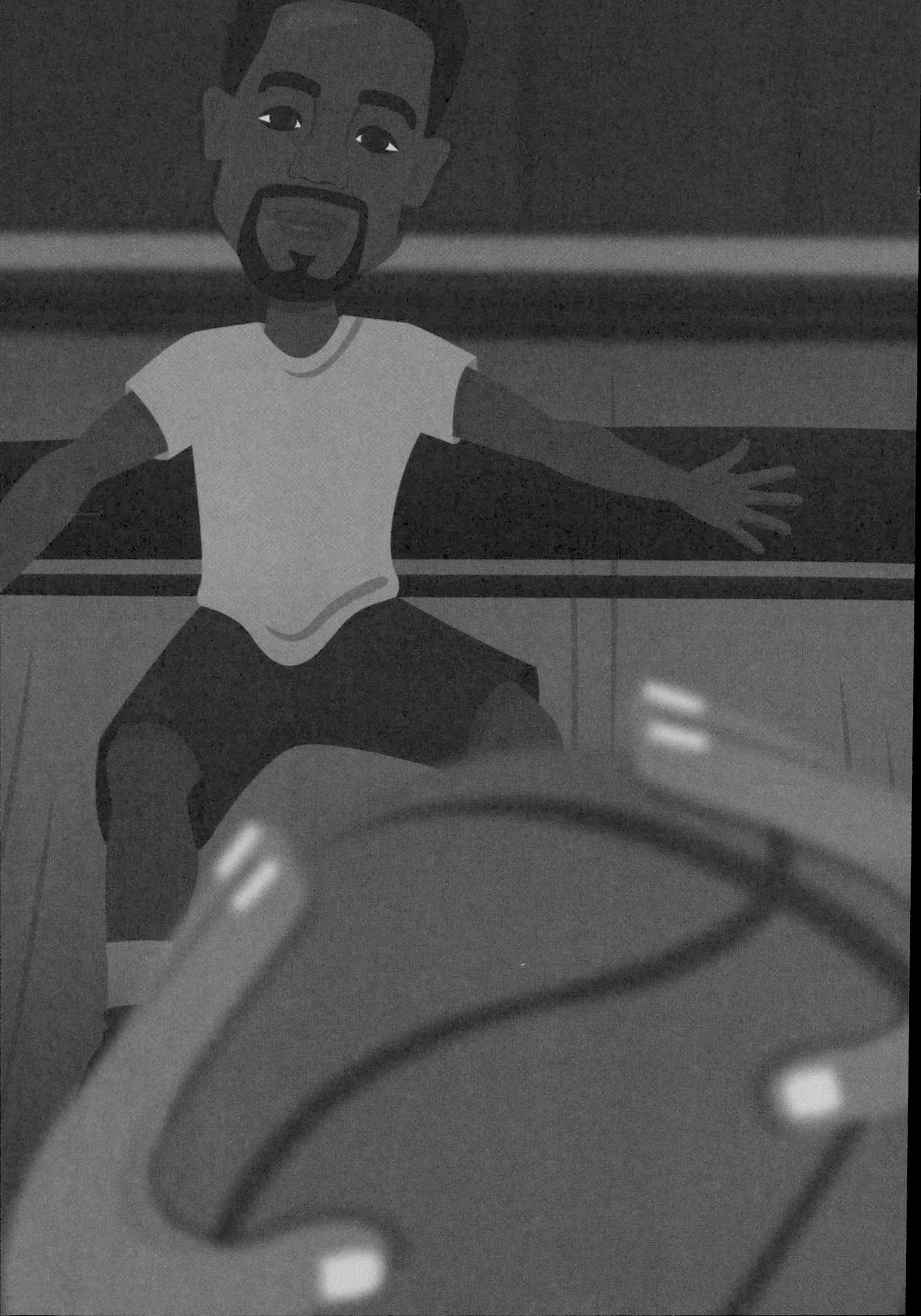

Chapter 17

Back to Earth

"Look at how nice this bus is!" Skylar says, as she loads her bags into the storage area.

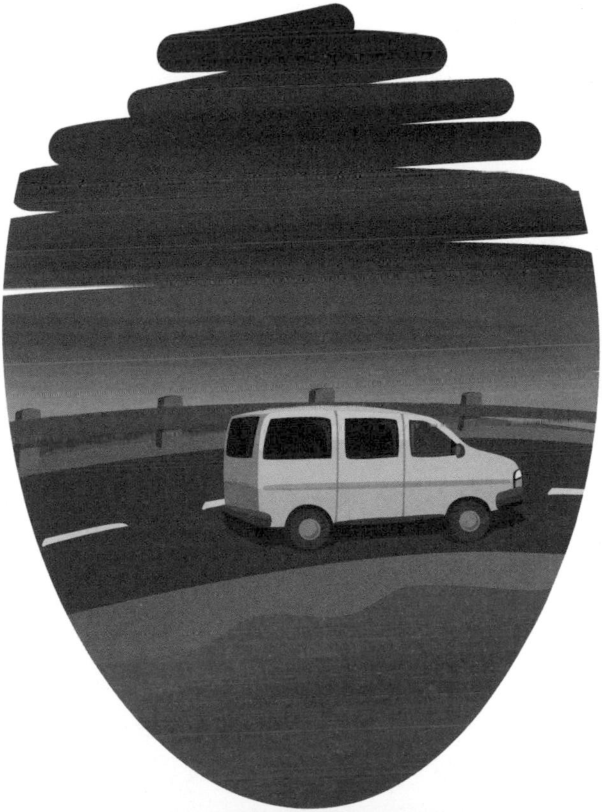

Ashley marvels at the sheer size of it and the sleek look because of the tinted windows. Inside, the seats are very soft and even *recline*, which means they fold up and down!

The girls have lots of fun on the ride down.

Skylar freestyle raps, making up lyrics packed with similes and metaphors about the Lady Soldiers and the titles they are going to win. Ashley provides the beat.

The girls tell funny stories, and they eat snacks like bulk bags of candy bars, chips, and fruit snacks. Time flies.

The next morning, the Lady Soldiers prepare for their first game. They play a team from Tennessee.

"All right, Family," Shalana says. "Win on 3."

"1...2...3...Win!"

The Tennessee team wins the tipoff. The point guard shoots and makes a three-pointer. The Lady Soldiers turn the ball over on their first possession, and the other team scores another three.

Daddymoe calls a timeout, with his team already down 6–0.

"All right," he says, "let's tighten up our defense."

The Lady Soldiers nod and return to the court.

Maybe we're just a little nervous, Skylar thinks.

More turnovers for the Soldiers, more layups and jumpers for the opponent.

Down 12–0, Shalana looks wide-eyed at Daddymoe. But on the next possession, Emily steals the ball, and passes to Skylar, who makes a layup.

The Lady Soldiers score!

In the game, though, the Lady Soldiers do not score nearly enough; they lose 32–12. The next game is not much better: a 42–24 loss to a team from Ohio.

Daddymoe's Rule

"Success does not happen overnight," Daddymoe says. "Progress is about getting a little better every day. Let's get better."

The Lady Soldiers play better in the next game, but they lose 36–24 to a team from North Carolina. Finally, in their fourth game, they beat a team from Nashville 40–33.

"It's a new day," Daddymoe says.

But the Lady Soldiers return to their dismal play like the start of the tournament. They suffer a 30-point loss to a team from an Atlanta suburb.

"We'll play against them again," Skylar vows.

On the bus ride back to South Bend, Daddymoe and his assistant coaches, P.D. and Steve, who drives the bus, discuss what they need to change to make the Lady Soldiers more successful.

"We've got to do something different," Daddymoe says.

Days later, Skylar sees that Daddymoe dresses differently for practice. Instead of his usual sweat pants and baseball hat, Daddymoe wears a sleeveless shirt, black shorts, and his basketball shoes.

P.D. and Steve are also ready to play.

The coaches decide they need to practice with the Lady Soldiers for them to improve. All three men are strong, so they collect most of the rebounds and score points in the paint.

On defense, they point out the players' weaknesses.

On Emily: "Make her shoot a pull up!" P.D. shouts.

On Ashley: "She can't hold onto the ball. She will drop it if you hit it!"

On Skylar: "I'll overplay her left," Daddymoe says. "She can't go right."

That makes Skylar upset. So, at home, Skylar practices dribbling with her right hand for 20 minutes before bedtime.

Over weeks, the Lady Soldiers get tougher, stronger, and better.

At a tournament not far from South Bend, the Lady Soldiers dominate and win the games by an average of 15 points. In the championship game, Skylar effortlessly scores 29 points. She is so good, she makes the game look simple.

The Lady Soldiers are growing and progressing. They are eager to go back to AAU National Championship.

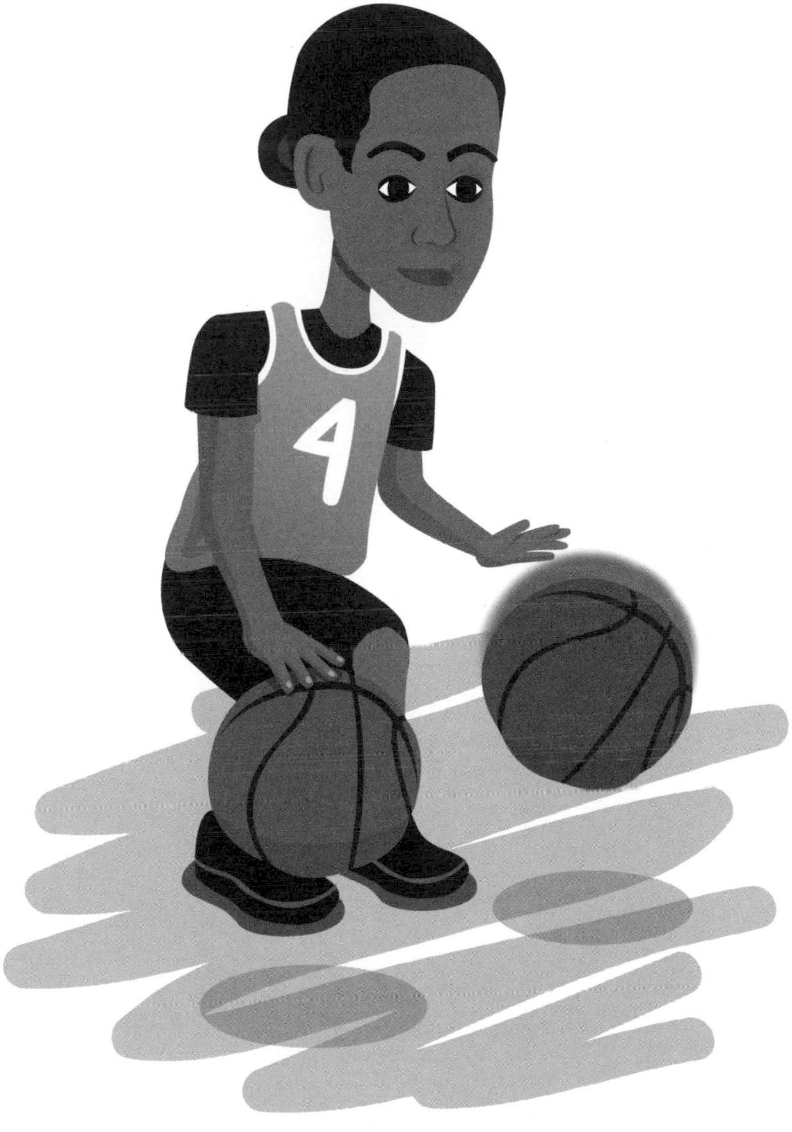
4

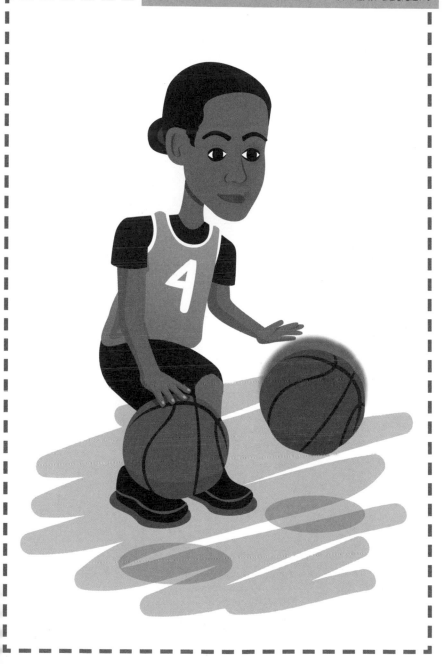

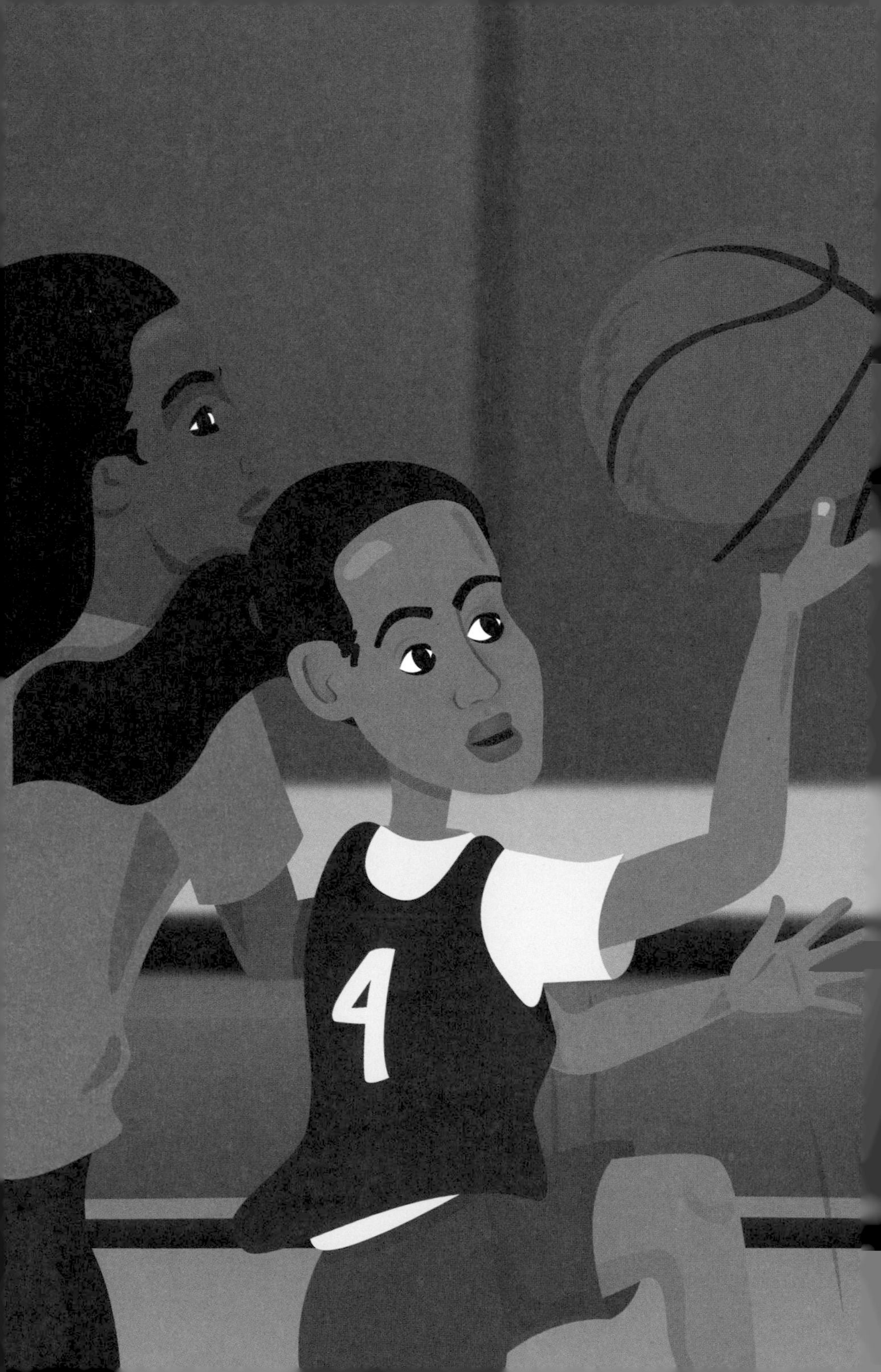

Chapter 18

Open Gym

"Daddymoe, where are we going?"

Skylar sits in the silver minivan behind Daddymoe, who is driving, and waits for an answer. Mom is in the passenger seat. Sitting behind her is Marcy, a talented, 16-year-old basketball player who Daddymoe trains at the King Center.

"We're driving to Indianapolis," Mom replies.

Skylar rolls her eyes. She loves to sing songs with her mom on drives in and around South Bend. But all the way to Indianapolis—two-and-a-half hours away? Skylar decides to take a nap instead.

"Wake up, Skylar," Daddymoe says, tapping her shoulder.

Still drowsy, Skylar opens her eyes and sees an unfamiliar gym. Marcy grabs her gym bag out of the trunk, so Skylar snatches hers too.

Skylar and Marcy follow Mom and Daddymoe toward the entrance. Once inside, two people welcome them.

"What class are you?" one woman asks Marcy.

"Class of 2003," Marcy says.

Skylar is confused. *There's a classroom in this gym?* she thinks.

"Fill this out," the woman says to Marcy, as she pushes forward a two-page form.

No one says a word to Skylar.

"Where's my class?" Skylar asks.

Everyone laughs.

"Oh, you're so cute," the woman replies. "Sure, you can fill out a form too."

Skylar smiles.

When she walks into the gym, she sees about 40 girls, all of them older—and taller—than her.

Daddymoe beelines toward Cousin Kevin. He runs a team called "The Family," and he coaches some of Indiana's best high school basketball players. He hosts an open workout and college coaches attend to scout the players, who are mostly sophomores and juniors.

Skylar starts to lace up her shoes.

"What are you doing, Skylar?" Mom asks.

"I'm getting ready to play," Skylar answers.

"Oh no you're not!" Mom says. "You're only 10 years old. Those girls are all bigger and older than you."

Skylar does not care.

Mom walks toward Kevin and Daddymoe.

"They are going to kill her," Mom says, pointing to one girl nearby who is 6 feet 3 inches. "Do not let her go out there."

But Kevin smiles.

"Actually, Skylar is the tenth player for one team," he says. "We need her."

Daddymoe nods.

Skylar is used to playing older girls, though not teenagers.

When the scrimmage starts, she does not dominate like she does in the Y league. But she plays point guard, and she makes smart passes and plays aggressive defense.

Skylar's mom winces when Skylar anticipates the direction of the opposing point guard and draws a *charge* near half court. That means the other player collects a foul, and Skylar's team gets the ball. The play showcases Skylar's fearlessness.

Though she only scores one basket, Skylar gets a few assists and two steals. Most important, though, her team wins the scrimmage.

"I had so much fun!" Skylar says to Kevin. "Thank you!"

Skylar's mom exhales. She is just glad that Skylar did not get hurt.

A few days later, Daddymoe calls Skylar to the dining room.

"I can't believe it," he says. "Look at this."

Daddymoe shows Skylar and Renee a letter.

"It's from Brenda Frese, the head coach at Ball State," he says as he skims the letter, which was on special paper. "She was at Kevin's event, and she wants us to know that she is going to be watching Skylar very closely."

Ball State is a public university in Muncie, Indiana, about two-and-a-half hours from South Bend.

"Can she do that?" Renee asks. "She's only in fifth grade!"

"It's called a letter of interest," Daddymoe says, "and they are perfectly legal."

Skylar's eyes light up.

She isn't even in middle school and a college is already interested in her.

This only makes Skylar hungrier to play basketball in college *and* in the WNBA.

After finishing her homework, Skylar heads to the backyard to practice dribbling with her right hand and make 100 baskets.

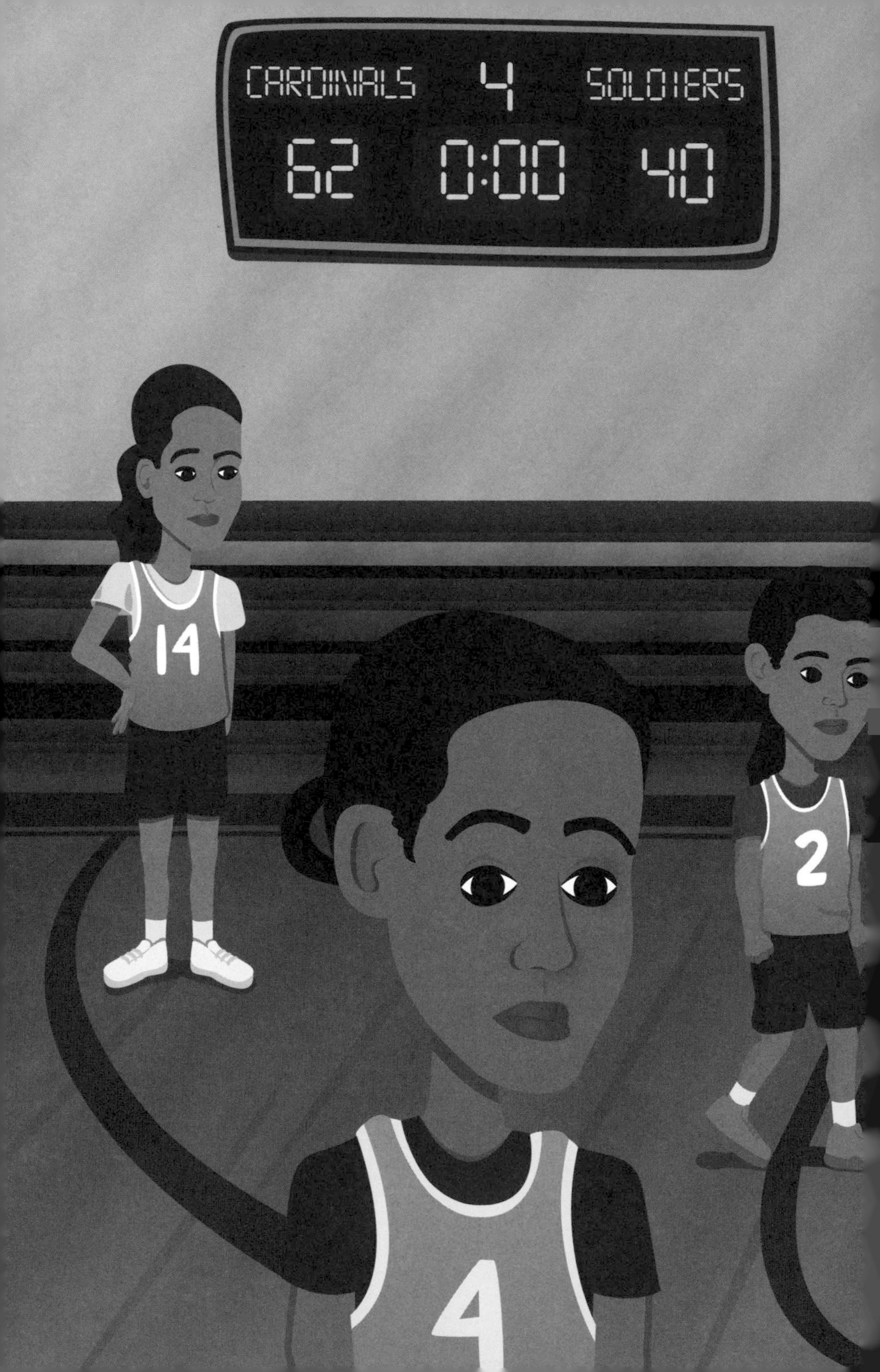
CARDINALS 4 SOLDIERS
62 0:00 40
14
2
4

Chapter 19

Watch and Learn

When Skylar is 11, the Lady Soldiers cruise to their region and state AAU titles. They qualify for the national tournament!

After another successful fundraiser, the girls want to enjoy one of the most fun cities in the world for kids: Orlando, Florida. That's even more special for Skylar because Orlando is only 90 minutes from Tampa, where Daddy and her brothers live!

The day before the Lady Soldiers' first game, some of the girls and their families go to a beach about an hour away. Some head to Disney World. Others shop at a big mall. Skylar has dinner and watches a movie with Daddy and her brothers who are excited about attending her games.

An hour before tip-off of the first game, Daddymoe does not sense the usual excitement from his players. Several Lady Soldiers yawn and lay around the locker room.

"All right, Family," Shalana says. "Win on 3."

"1...2...3...Win."

The cheer lacks its usual gusto.

When they walk on the court, though, the Lady Soldiers marvel at the stands. They see a sea of fans wearing red shirts featuring the same logo as the jerseys of their opponent. They are from Louisville, and their fans stomp and sing loudly.

"Who rocks this house?" one father yells.

"The Cardinals rock this house!" dozens of others scream.

They do this over and over.

The Lady Soldiers do not start well, and they do not rally. The Cardinals steamroll them, 62–40.

In the locker room, Daddymoe is usually positive and upbeat, even when they lose. But today he is upset—and he sends them a strong message.

"I know Orlando has beaches, theme parks, and malls," he says quietly, "and those things are a lot of fun. But we came here to play basketball! If we lose tomorrow, we're going home."

The girls all lock their eyes on Daddymoe. The way the national tournament is set up means a team could lose a few games and still advance to the championship. But Daddymoe makes clear another poor performance will mean a quick trip home.

Daddymoe's Rule

"We are not going to waste your family's hard-earned money," Daddymoe says. "Tune out the distractions and focus on the number one goal of this trip."

The girls accept the message. Instead of going to a team dinner at a theme park, they decide to eat next to their hotel and rest in their rooms.

When he does bed checks, Daddymoe notices Skylar intently watching the television.

When he steps into the room, Daddymoe also sees her scribbling down notes.

"What are you doing, Skylar?" he asks.

Skylar peeks up.

"Oh, I'm watching the tape of our game," she says.

Skylar continues her film study. She replays the moves of her opponent, a taller but faster guard, over and over and over again.

She looks for clues in the tape to see why her opponent scored on her with nifty post moves near the basket. Skylar searches for tips on why she misses three layups. She discovers that the Cardinal guard would stick her hands in Skylar's face when she leaps toward the rim.

"Since she is bigger, what can I do to create more space between us?" Skylar asks herself.

Daddymoe smiles, stands, and heads for the door.

"How long have you been watching tape?" he asks Skylar before leaving.

"About an hour," Skylar says, "but I only have 20 more minutes, then I'll go to bed."

Skylar learns some things she can do better the next time she plays against a taller and faster opponent. But she wishes she were home, so she could head to her backyard court to practice before bed. Their hotel, unfortunately, does not have a basket.

At the next game, the Lady Soldiers regain their confidence and their energy. They blow out a team from Dallas, and they convincingly defeat each opponent until they reach the championship game.

Though Skylar scores 29 points, the Lady Soldiers lose by eight points to a team from Atlanta.

At the medal ceremony, each of the Lady Soldiers graciously accepts their hammer-sized, second-place trophies. They are proud of how much they have improved in a year.

But they are not satisfied.

They want the three-tiered championship trophy, which must be handled with *both* hands.

"That would look really sweet at the King Center," Skylar whispers to Emily.

"Next year," Emily answers.

Daddy, Shay, Dezz, and Tayta walk from the stands to the court, where they hug Skylar.

"Great job, Skylar," Daddy says. "You were amazing!"

The Lady Soldiers return to the King Center and keep practicing and playing against boys their age and even men. Ashley grows stronger and stronger, both physically and mentally. Em develops a reliable jump shot, and Skylar finishes better around the hoop.

The Lady Soldiers lose a lot of practice games to the boys and men. But they keep growing individually and collectively and push for the next win.

Then something clicks.

The Lady Soldiers put everything together, and they start to dominate opponents on the court. At the next AAU National Championship, Skylar leads the way, as the Soldiers win the title, defeating every team, including the one from Atlanta that beat them the previous year.

The Lady Soldiers' family-first approach and their years of hard work pay off.

They are champions!

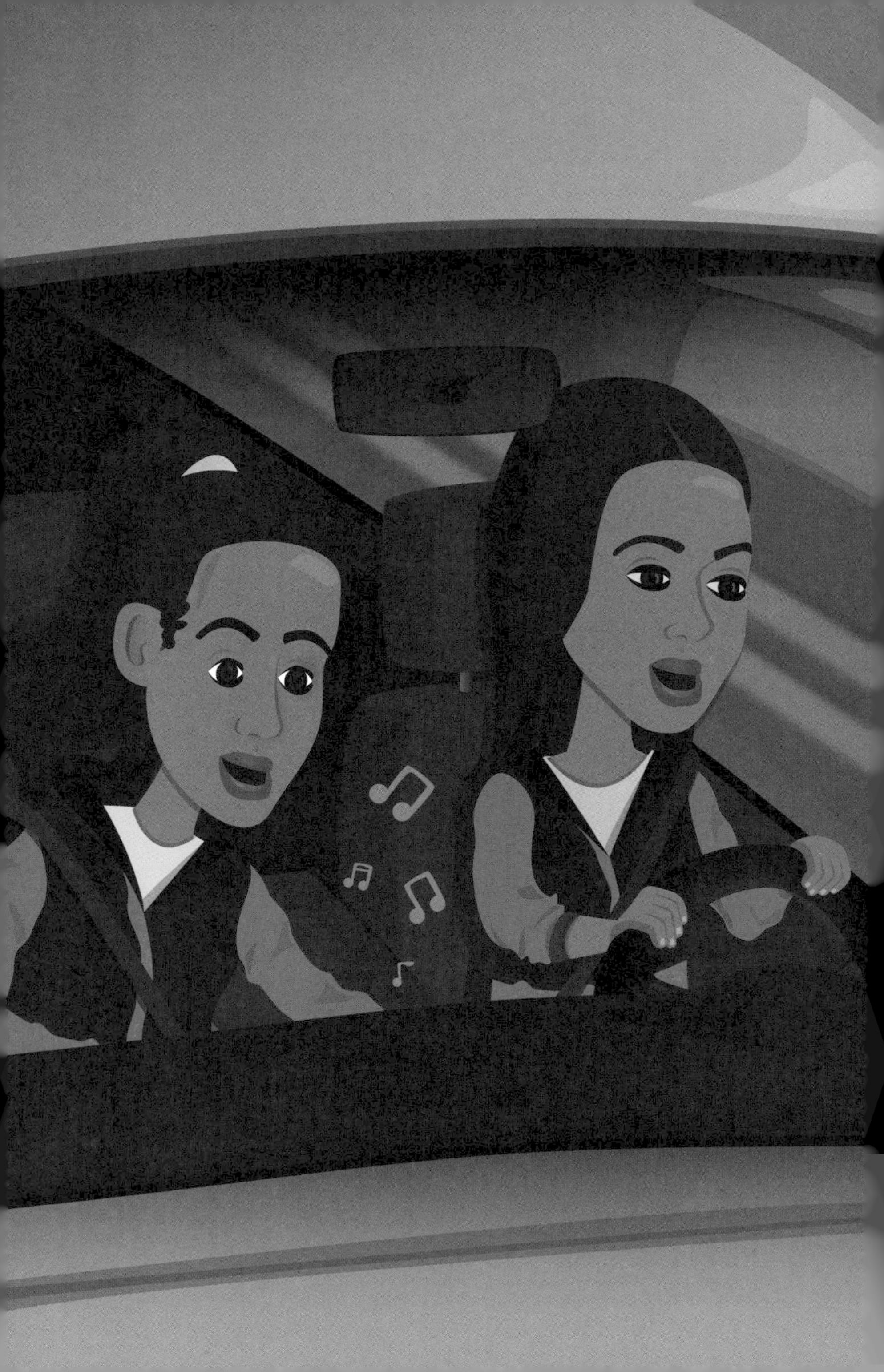

Chapter 20

Renee's Rules

Skylar gets so much from her mom. Like her taste in music.

They love to ride in the silver car and sing along to 90s Rhythm & Blues (also known as R&B) music, especially female groups like TLC, SWV, Xscape, En Vogue and Destiny's Child. They bond as they belt out lyrics to the latest songs.

Skylar is close to her mom. They often record silly messages on their answering machine. Before cell phones, telephones were connected to an electronic device that enabled a person to record a message for someone who couldn't pick up the call.

"Sorry, we're not home right now," Skylar says.

"So leave a message," Mom says, "and we'll get back..."

Skylar sings, "To you."

Then Mom sings, "To you."

Skylar and her mom sometimes dress alike, wearing matching Starter jackets of professional teams. Mom affectionately calls Skylar "Mini-me."

Skylar also gets her competitive spirit from her mom. The family tries to play board games, but Mom occasionally—out of frustration—refuses to officially finish a game. Mom doesn't like to lose.

Once, Skylar sets Mom up in Connect Four. No matter where Mom puts her red disc, Skylar wins with her next move because she planned two ways to win.

Realizing this, Mom insists on switching to another board game.

"Let's play Monopoly!" Mom says.

"But Mom, I'm about to win," Skylar replies.

"No, no," Mom says, as she slides the release valve so all the discs fall down. "We didn't finish. Who knows what would have happened?"

That makes Skylar a little upset, but she is too respectful to protest. Besides, Daddymoe winks and smiles at Skylar, subtly congratulating her on the inevitable win.

Mom does not excel in board games. But she is the family's best bowler, averaging a score of 165 out of 300. That's really good!

The family goes to Chippewa Bowl every few weeks, and Mom usually dominates. She takes bowling seriously. She owns her own bowling shoes and a light green ball with *Renee* etched into it by the finger holes.

Mom always goes last, so she can see how many pins she needs to win a game.

One Friday night, Daddymoe gets into a groove and gets a couple of *strikes*—when you knock down all 10 pins with your first roll of the ball—and many *spares*—when you knock down all 10 pins with two rolls.

Daddymoe builds a 15-pin lead on Mom in the tenth and final frame of the game. Mom grabs her light green ball, positions herself, and walks toward the bowling lane. She releases the ball, which hurtles forward then slams onto the hard, wooden floor. The ball rolls and rolls then crashes into the pins.

The white pins fly all over but one remains standing. It is Mom's least favorite, the 10-pin, which is the one furthest to the right. Because she spins the ball, she has to throw her ball *just so* to knock that pin down.

Mom grabs her ball, takes a deep breath, and walks toward the pins. She releases the ball, which rolls and rolls, then barely bumps the 10-pin into the gutter. She gets her spare!

On her final ball, Mom needs just six pins to beat Daddymoe. Given her bowling skill, Mom does that easily, actually toppling nine pins.

Mom wins!

Daddymoe wants to win, but he is sort of relieved: a few months earlier, Mom refused to ride home with him after he defeated her in mini golf.

Mom is not only competitive in sports and board games. She is competitive with schoolwork. When Skylar can read and write, Mom gets her daughter books and workbooks.

In second grade, Skylar sits in the kitchen and works on math word problems. She reads and re-reads the final one.

"I can't..." Skylar starts to say.

But Mom does not let her finish.

Mom's Rule

"Listen to me, Skylar," Mom says. "We do not use the word *can't* in this house. Instead, we say, 'I'll try.' Someone will help you if you're willing to try instead of complaining or quitting."

Skylar takes a deep breath.

"Mom, I am trying to solve this final math problem," Skylar says, "but I need your help."

"That's better," Mom says.

They read the problem together, and Mom asks Skylar a few questions. Mom does not give Skylar the answer but instead prompts her to look at the problem in a different way.

"Oh, I see!" Skylar exclaims, finding a new perspective to solve the problem. She furiously writes the answer on her math sheet, and proudly looks up.

"Thanks, Mom!"

They hug.

Mom comes to terms with the fact that Skylar does not want to participate in the childhood activities she once enjoyed like gymnastics and cheerleading. But Skylar appreciates her mom's constant support and always looks for a special sign before each game. Because they are often in loud gyms, Mom uses sign language to encourage Skylar.

Before a game starts, Skylar searches the stands and locates her mom.

Mom spells out U-D-O-U. *You do you.*

She's done that since Skylar was six years old!

It's her reminder for Skylar to be herself, not to measure her success based on anyone else, and not to let others control her emotions.

Skylar *needs* to see Mom's signal; it gives her peace and confidence.

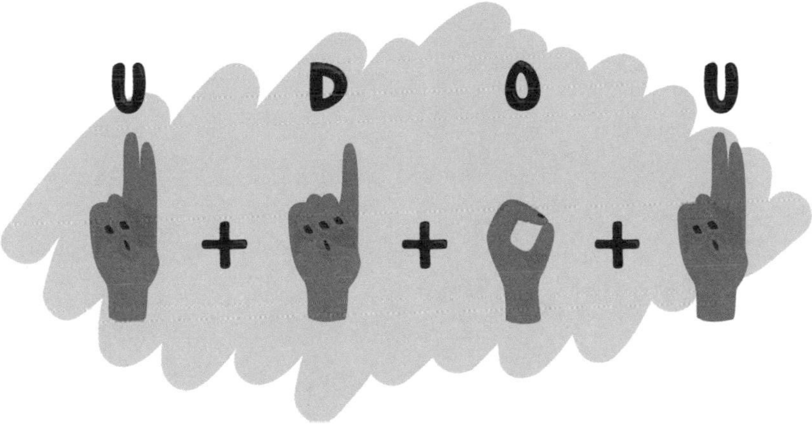
U
D
O
U
+
+
+

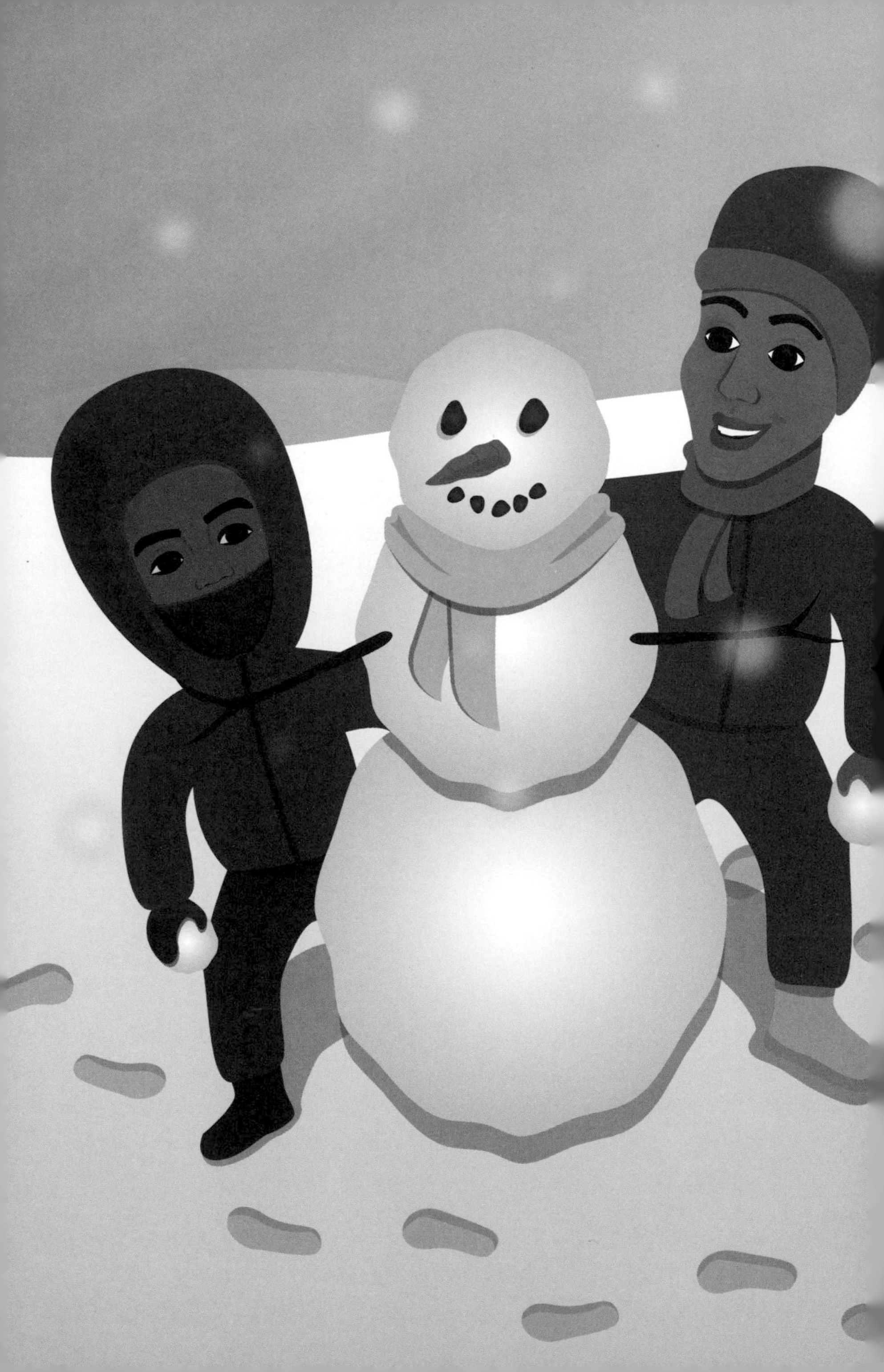

Chapter 21

Big Sister

Skylar takes three things seriously: her studies, her hoops, and her siblings.

Skylar is a big sister to one girl, Haneefah, and three boys: Dezz, Tayta, and Junior. Haneefah lives with her mom in Chicago, and Dezz and Tayta live with Daddy in Florida.

<u>Daddy's Rule</u>

"You have an important responsibility," Daddy says. "When you are the oldest, you must set a good example."

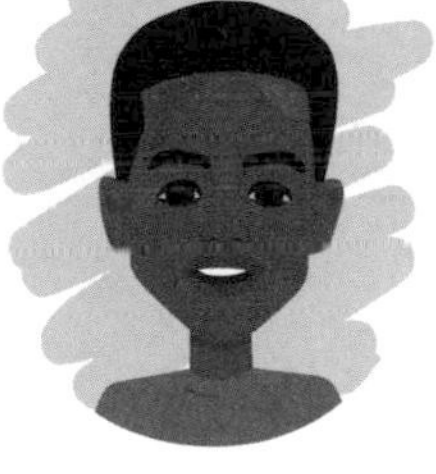

Junior is Mom and Daddymoe's son, and he lives with Skylar. He looks up to his sister and follows her everywhere. Skylar, who is eight years older, does not mind.

But when he starts to talk at two years old, Junior says some words over and over again. At three, Junior repeats certain syllables, words, and phrases and sometimes drags out sounds. Mom and Daddymoe take Junior to a specialist who diagnoses Junior with a speech disorder called *stuttering*.

It is a common challenge for many young children under the age of five. But other kids, including cousins, are not always kind.

Junior is the youngest of all his cousins. When they are bored, the cousins often pick on Junior because his stuttering is especially bad when he is frustrated or angry.

"Stop it!" Skylar yells at her cousins. "Leave him alone!"

Mom and Daddymoe can calm Junior down and get him to communicate his thoughts. But no one can connect with Junior like his big sister. At Halloween, while her friends sprint from house to house to collect lots of candy, Skylar holds Junior's hand and walks at his speed. Afterwards, she helps him sort the candy: chocolates in one pile, lollipops in another, and hard candies like Gobstoppers in a third pile.

When Junior struggles with his speech, Skylar gets down on one knee, gently holds his face with her hands, and looks him in the eyes.

"Slow down," Skylar softly says to Junior. "Tell me what's on your mind."

Junior settles down, takes a deep breath, and speaks clearly to Skylar.

One Sunday afternoon, when Junior is five years old, his cousins bother him so much that he says a naughty word.

Nana, who is Daddymoe's mother, is upstairs. She hears the word and yells, "What did you say?"

The kids can hear her walking down the hallway, toward the stairs. Nana picks up a wooden spoon when the kids act up. That means Nana is not playing around.

"Do you want me to pop you on the knuckles?" Nana says.

Cussing, or saying a word you are not supposed to, can get you a spanking with the spoon.

Skylar does not want Junior to get hit with Nana's spoon, so she rushes to the kitchen, grabs it, and tosses it into the wood-burning stove.

A moment later, Nana storms into the kitchen.

"Where is my spoon?" Nana loudly says. "I know it's around here somewhere!"

None of the cousins tell on Skylar because they do not like the spoon either.

After 10 minutes, Nana gives up looking for her spoon. During that time, she calms down and decides to show Junior mercy.

"Junior, you're lucky I can't find my spoon," Nana says. "Now don't let me hear naughty words out of your mouth again!"

Skylar tries to help Junior and does exercises with him before dinnertime.

On a snowy day, Daddymoe, Skylar, and Junior play outside. They build a snowman together and name him Ray Ray. The kids pretend to play a hide-and-seek game with him.

"See, Ray Ray is having fun," Skylar says to her little brother. "But he's not talking too fast. You got it?"

As Skylar puts the scarf on Ray Ray, Daddymoe pelts her with a snowball.

"Oh, it's on now!" Skylar says.

Seconds later, Junior repeats what his sister says—and he does so without stuttering!

"Oh, it's on now!" Junior excitedly says.

It's a special moment for Daddymoe. He's proud of Junior *and* Skylar.

After a 10-minute snowball fight, the three of them go inside, where Mom has hot cocoa with marshmallows ready.

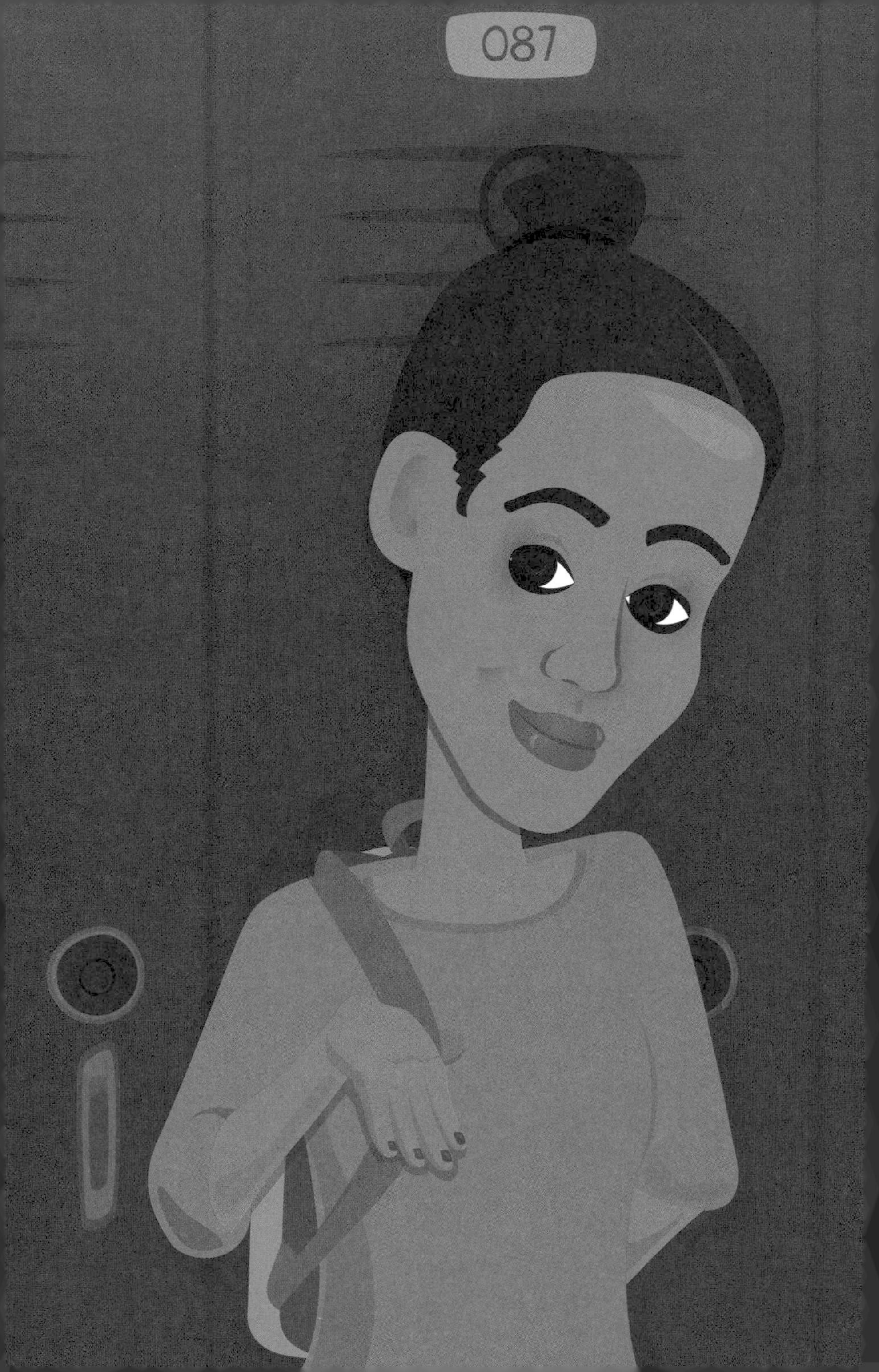
087

Chapter 22 Beauty and the Beast

Because she is so good at basketball, Skylar plays *up*, which means her teammates are usually one or two years older. When she is in seventh grade, Skylar's teammates are already in high school!

Skylar wears sweat pants, t-shirts or jerseys, and gym shoes to school every day. She also puts her hair in a ponytail. For two years, Skylar needs braces for her teeth. She needs cleansers and treatments for *acne*—a skin condition that results in bumps and inflamed spots, usually on a person's face.

How Skylar looks is very different from the way her teammates look. No one on the team is more stylish than Ashley, who wears dresses and styles her hair in an array of ways.

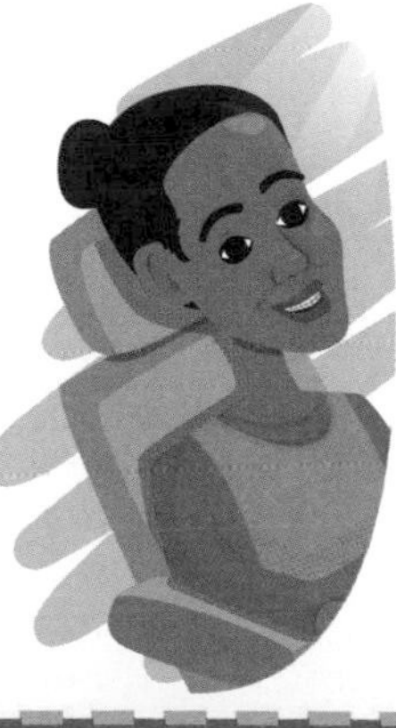

Just before basketball season in seventh grade, Skylar gets her braces taken off at the orthodontist's office. An *orthodontist* is a dentist who specializes in straightening crooked teeth.

"Are you excited, Skylar?" Dr. Ben asks. "Are you ready for me to remove the braces after two years?"

Skylar nods. She is not afraid.

Dr. Ben tells her exactly what he will do to remove her braces: He will use pliers to help remove the metal brackets in her mouth, and then he'll use a metal scraper to clean her teeth. After that, Dr. Ben will put a mold in her mouth for her retainer, which she will wear at night to help hold her teeth in the right position.

"This will take an hour," Dr. Ben tells Skylar.

The whole thing is a breeze!

Without her braces, Skylar looks and *feels* different, especially now that her acne is also clearing. After a few days, Skylar decides she wants to make more changes.

New hairdos, new clothes, new shoes.

Skylar's friends do not pressure her to change; Skylar, nonetheless, feels pressure to change.

"Mom, I want to start buying my own clothes," Skylar says at dinner. "Can I have some money so I can go shopping with Ashley and Em?"

The request surprises Daddymoe and Mom, but they agree and give her money. Usually, every few months when there's a sale, they go to a sporting goods store and buy Skylar a few new pair of athletic pants, shirts, and shoes.

What will she wear now?

Skylar starts to look at magazines for teenage girls, and she pays more attention to the television commercials for girls. She trades in her basketball gear for sandals, floral dresses, and hair accessories.

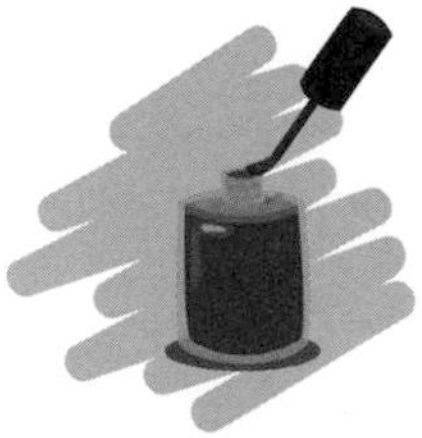

Skylar wants to be a beast on the court but a beauty off it. Months pass, though, and Skylar does not *feel* any better.

"Mom, can I ask you something?" Skylar says before bedtime.

"Of course," Mom replies.

"I want to fit in, and I'm tired of girls at school calling me a tomboy," Skylar says. "I don't want to be 'one of the guys.'"

Skylar shares with her mom that she does not feel comfortable in her new clothes, and she does not like to go shopping.

"It's just so hard to keep up with all the fashion trends," Skylar says.

Mom puts her right arm on Skylar's shoulder.

Mom's Rule

"Don't you pay attention to those magazines or commercials," Mom says. "And don't you pay attention to what anyone else says or does. You are beautiful just as you are, no matter what you do with your hair or what you wear. Just be yourself."

The next day, Skylar puts her hair in a ponytail and slides into sweat pants.

"Ahhhh," she says, "just right!"

One girl makes a rude comment at school, but Skylar cares more about the reaction of her teammates.

After school, Skylar heads to the King Center, where the Lady Soldiers will practice. She sees Em and Ashley.

"What's up, girl?" Em says to Skylar.

"I tried, but I don't like getting all dressed up," Skylar says. "I missed my sweats and sneakers."

Ashley shrugs her shoulders.

"That's cool, Skylar," she says. "Whatever makes you comfortable. You're still our girl, either way!"

Finally Skylar feels free.

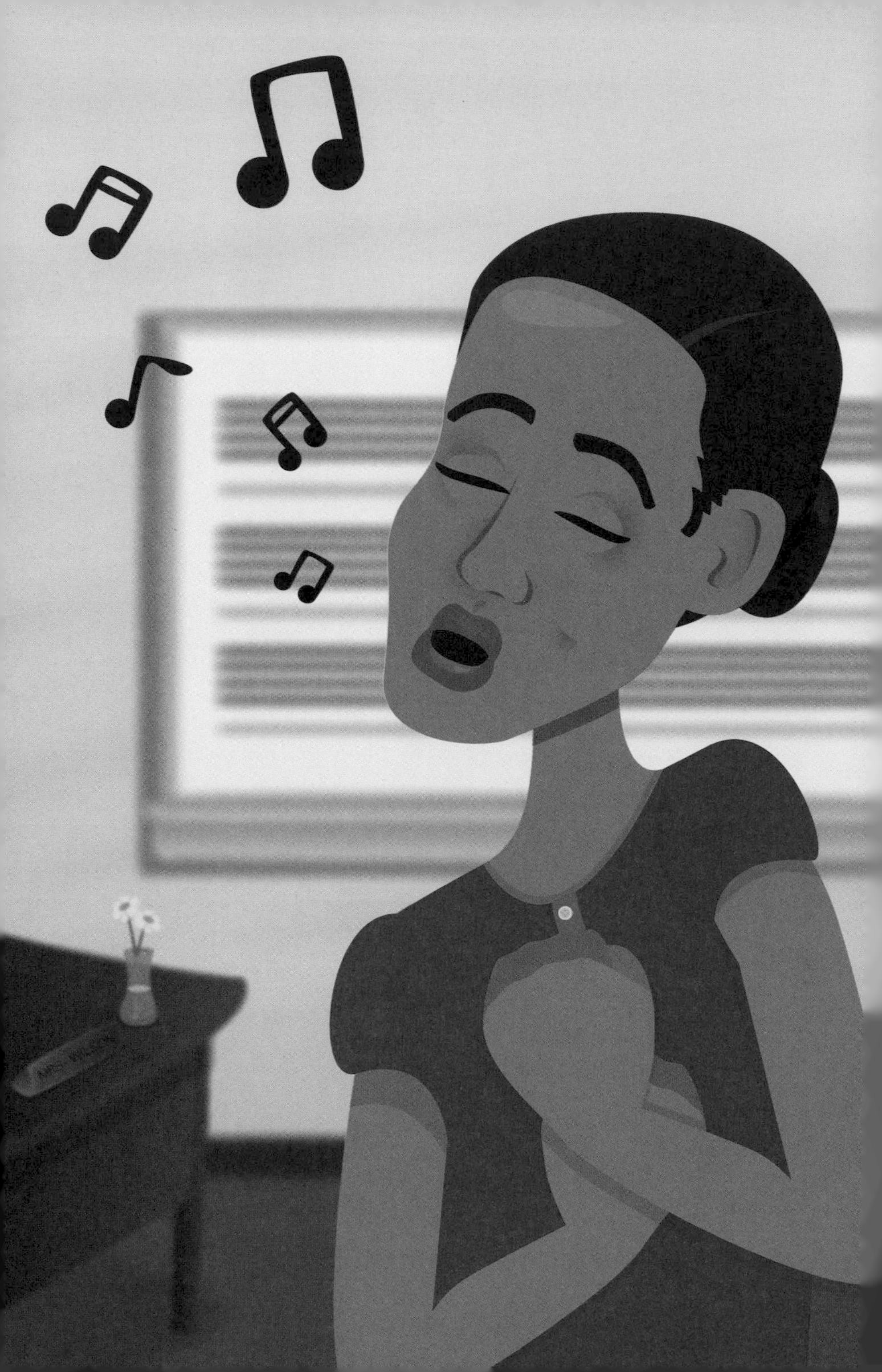

Chapter 23

Mrs. Wilson

Eighth grade is a challenging year for Skylar. She wrestles with how to dress, how to relate to classmates her age, and how to handle her growing popularity as a star basketball player.

Her overall success is a *double-edged sword*, something that is both good and bad. People recognize Skylar for thriving in sports and academics. But people do not acknowledge her hard work: the hours she spends refining her basketball skills in the backyard, or the extra effort she puts forth in subjects like art and music. Skylar would not excel if she did not practice so much.

That's why Skylar is especially grateful for her choir teacher.

Mrs. Wilson has a presence about her, a special magnetism that deeply connects her to her students. Her classroom is at the end of a hallway, and students frequently visit her between classes.

Skylar is among Mrs. Wilson's regulars. She appreciates that she can tell Mrs. Wilson anything and that her teacher never judges her. Mrs. Wilson is kind and wise, mostly listening and only offering advice when Skylar specifically asks.

Mrs. Wilson reminds Skylar of Granny Stella. After she chats with Mrs. Wilson, Skylar *always* feels better! Mrs. Wilson even attends some of Skylar's basketball games.

But with Christmas approaching, Skylar debates whether to try out for a concert solo. Skylar *loves* to sing in the car with her mom or on the bus with her teammates. But she doesn't know if she's good enough to sing on a stage in front of classmates and strangers. Skylar thinks there are two girls in choir who have a better voice than she does.

"Mrs. Wilson, I have a question for you," Skylar says after class.

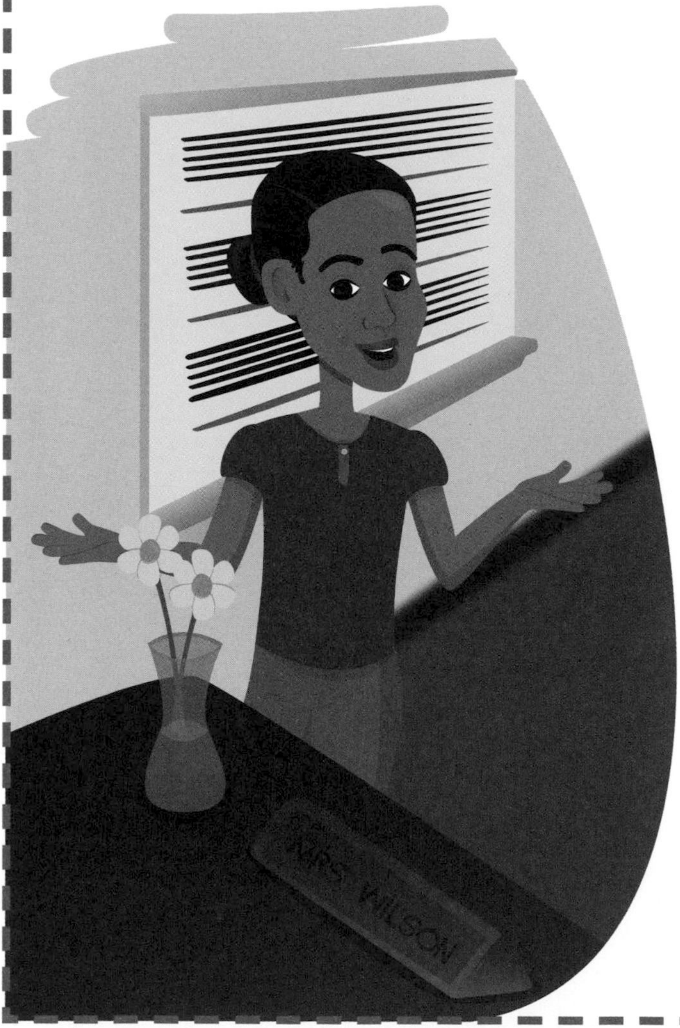
MRS. WILSON

"What is it, dear?" Mrs. Wilson replies.

"I want to sing *Sleigh Ride* for the Christmas concert, but I don't know if I'm good enough," Skylar says.

Mrs. Wilson smiles.

Mrs. Wilson's Rule

"It's better to try and fail," Mrs. Wilson says, "then to fail to try. If you don't try, you'll never grow."

Skylar decides to try.

"Thanks, Mrs. Wilson!" she says.

"You have a lovely voice," Mrs. Wilson says. "Just make sure you practice. The *jingle-ing, ring-ting-tingle-ing* can be tricky!"

Skylar memorizes the words to *Sleigh Ride*, and she makes Mom play the version of the song by The Ronettes: a female trio from New York who were popular in the 1960s. She practices singing the song before bed and after she wakes up.

Skylar does not feel nervous playing basketball in a gymnasium packed with fans, but she does feel nervous about singing in an auditorium filled with parents, teachers, and classmates.

Once again, Skylar's extra practice pays off. She passionately sings the song, *and* she nails the part Mrs. Wilson warned her about!

"Congratulations, Skylar!" Mrs. Wilson says afterwards. "That was wonderful!"

Skylar is glad that she was not afraid to try.

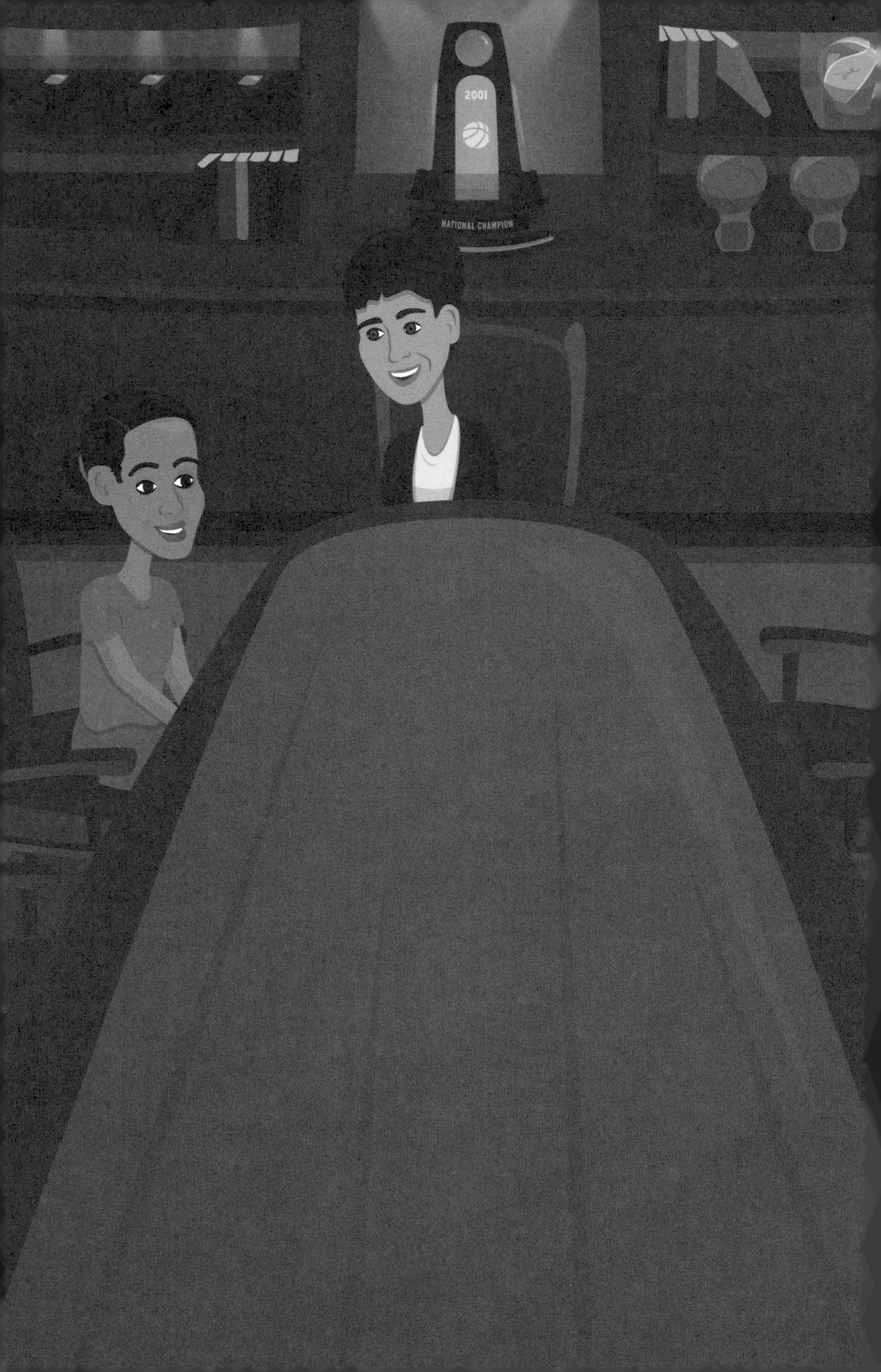
2001
NATIONAL CHAMPION

Chapter 24

The Offer

In her final eighth grade basketball game, Skylar scores 32 points and leads her middle school team to a convincing win. Afterwards, a college coach approaches Mom and Daddymoe.

"Your daughter is very good," the college coach says.

"Thank you," Mom says politely.

"I don't usually give scholarships to girls from the inner-city," the coach continues. "They have problems adjusting to the academics at my school. But I may have to make an exception for Skylar."

"Excuse me?" Mom says.

"Thank you and good luck," Daddymoe says, as he politely steers Mom away from the conversation.

Like Mom, Daddymoe is offended by the coach's *prejudiced* comment—that means saying something unkind about someone based on presumption, not facts or reasons. It bothers Mom and Daddymoe because they raise Skylar to be a scholar first and then an athlete.

Daddymoe's Rule
"Let the haters hate," Daddymoe says. "We'll just keep rolling."

The coach may or may not be *hating*, but Skylar does not have time to educate or fix everyone.

THE OFFER

In the spring, dozens of college basketball coaches attend an AAU tournament in Monroe, Louisiana. The Lady Soldiers advance to the quarterfinals, and Skylar averages 18 points and eight rebounds per game.

When the tournament ends, a female coach approaches Daddymoe and Mom. Skylar does not immediately recognize her, but Daddymoe and Mom do.

"Hello, my name is Muffet McGraw, and I coach at Notre Dame. I'd like your family to come visit us on campus and have a conversation with us about Skylar's future," Coach McGraw says.

She hands Mom a business card.

"What do you think, Skylar?" Daddymoe asks.

"That sounds like fun," Skylar says.

Daddymoe is an assistant coach on the Washington High School girls' basketball team, and he knows college coaches do not regularly invite middle-school players to visit campus.

Ten days later, Skylar, Daddymoe, Mom, and Junior make the short drive to Notre Dame's sprawling campus. The buildings are old but beautiful, and the grounds are plush with green grass and manicured bushes and trees.

Coach McGraw leads Skylar and her family on a tour of the facilities, including the court at the Joyce Center. At center court is a big, blue *N* intertwined with a *D*.

Skylar cannot believe she's *standing* on the court that the 2001 championship team played on!

Other than 2001, though, the Notre Dame women's basketball program has not consistently contended for a title. Connecticut, Stanford, and Tennessee are among the powerhouse programs.

At the dining hall, Skylar enjoys the broad selection of foods and treats. Mom lets her get whatever she wants; it's a special day!

To finish the visit, Coach McGraw invites Skylar and her family into a massive conference room. Skylar has never seen a bigger television or conference table. In the middle of the table is a telephone with a lot of buttons.

"We make a lot of important calls on that phone," Coach McGraw says. She invites everyone to take a seat but asks Skylar to sit next to her.

"Skylar, I have watched you play quite a few games," Coach McGraw says. "I really like your passion for the game and how smart and competitive you are on the court. You really want to be great, don't you?"

Skylar nods and says, "Yes, ma'am."

"I think you're a special young lady, and I think you have a lot of potential as a leader," Coach McGraw continues. "That's why I'm going to do something I've never done."

Daddymoe inches forward in his seat, curious to hear what Coach McGraw is going to say. Skylar has no clue what the coach has in mind.

"I would like to offer you an athletic scholarship to play basketball at Notre Dame," Coach McGraw says.

Daddymoe's eyes get big, and Mom's mouth opens in shock.

THE OFFER

Colleges charge students *tuition*, a sum of money for their education. Most students can earn a degree—or a specialty—from a college in four years. That can be very expensive, especially at a school like Notre Dame. But some colleges offer special students a *scholarship*—money toward their education—to come to their campus.

A full athletic scholarship meant Skylar would attend Notre Dame four years for free!

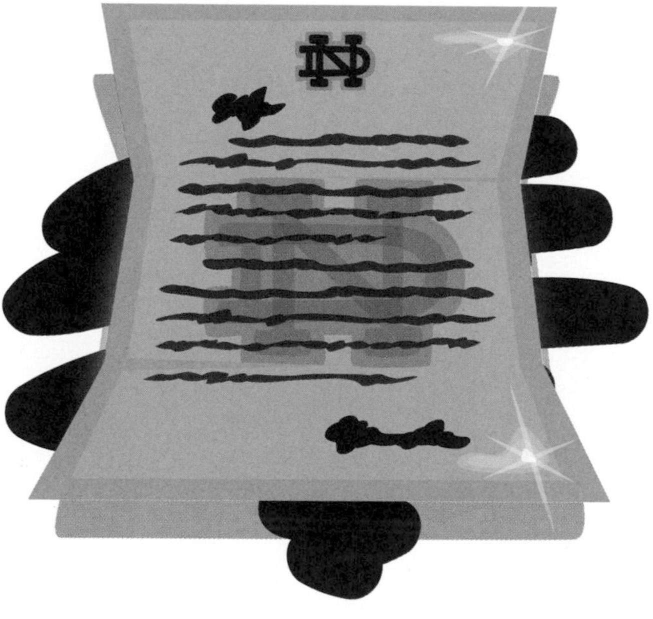

Moments pass.

"Oh thank you," Skylar finally says. "This is so flattering."

In college sports, Division I is the highest level, and schools are able to offer a certain number of student-athlete scholarships. Usually, a college offers a high school athlete a scholarship during his or her junior year. As soon as a college makes an offer, a student-athlete can provide a verbal commitment. Nothing is official, though, until the student-athlete signs a National Letter of Intent with a college or university.

Skylar wants to keep her options open.

"I have some things to think about," Skylar tells Coach McGraw and rises from her plush, leather swivel chair.

Coach McGraw had hoped Skylar would verbally commit to Notre Dame, but she is impressed with Skylar's composure and maturity.

"Well, I want to thank you for coming to visit with me," Coach McGraw says. "Best of luck in high school."

Skylar and her family make their way to the parking lot and climb inside their car.

"Can you believe this?" Daddymoe says once his car door closes. "Coach McGraw offers you a scholarship, and you say you've got some things to think about? Are you kidding me?" Daddymoe laughs.

During the visit, Skylar tried hard to be serious and mature and control her emotions. But in the car, Skylar screams and smiles.

Mom beams with pride.

A few in the family had started college but no one had graduated, sometimes because they did not have enough money to pay for the education. Skylar could be the first.

"You haven't even played a high school game yet," Mom says, "and Coach McGraw offered you a scholarship."

"I can't believe it," Skylar says.

But once the family gets home, Skylar heads to the backyard. She's got a lot of work to do.

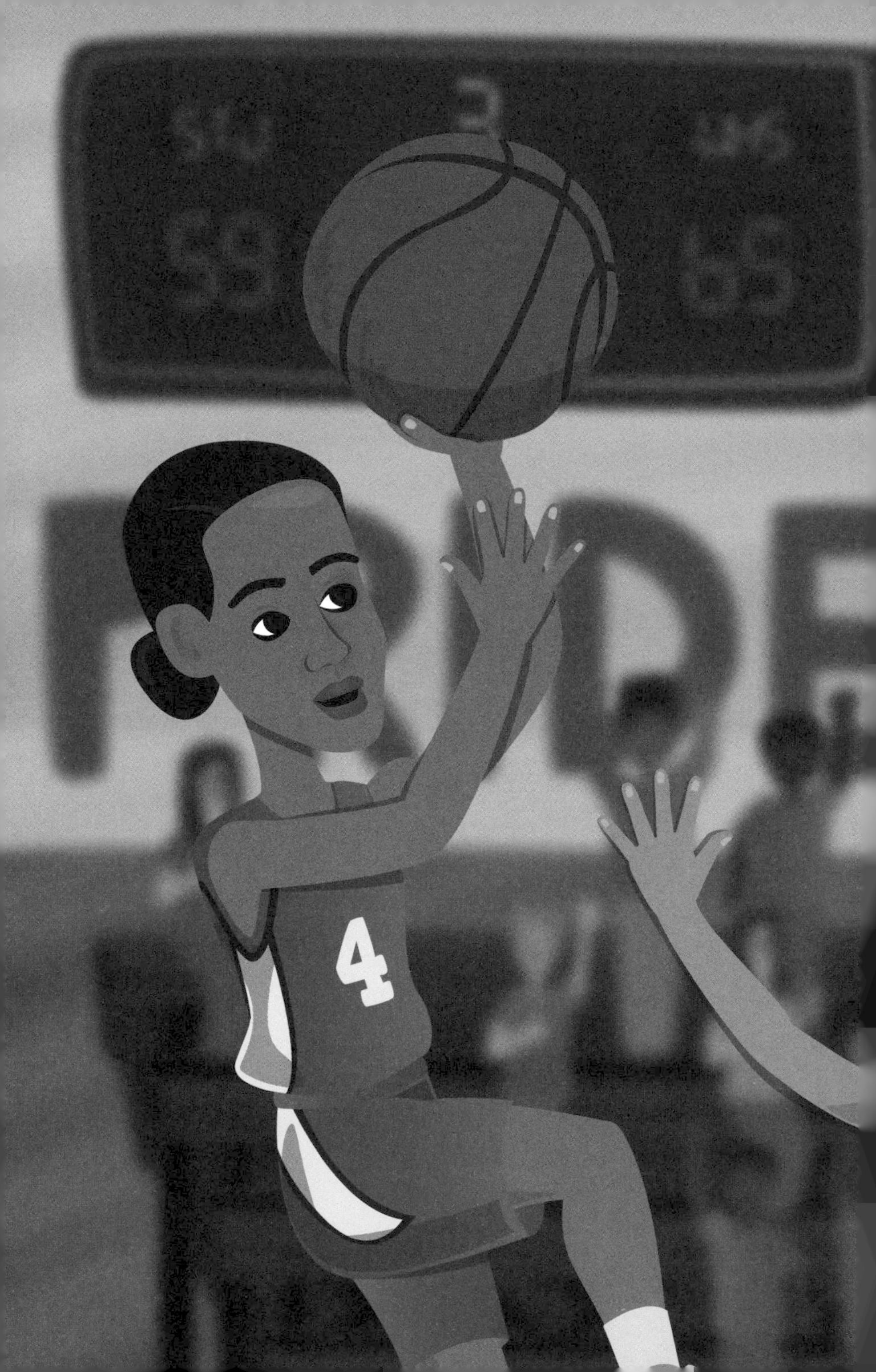
4

Chapter 25

The Underdogs

The transition from middle to high school is tough. Skylar has learned a lot of good rules for life, and she has one more advantage: Daddymoe is a girls' basketball coach at Washington High School. Skylar already knows the hallways, and she knows where the big gym and the small gym are. She's happy, too, because the Panthers girls' basketball team has a good reputation, winning a few conference titles and producing college athletes like Jacqueline Batteast, who would go on to shine at Notre Dame.

Freshman do not normally play on the varsity team. But Skylar is not a normal freshman. She has a starting spot on the team.

In her first three games, she scores 27, 30, and 25 points. Dozens of family members attend every game, as is their custom.

Some female classmates are not impressed.

"Those teams were terrible," a classmate named Nina says to Skylar. "I bet you won't score that many points against St. Joe's."

St. Joseph's is the defending state champion and star player Melissa Lechlitner is headed to Notre Dame after her high school graduation. ESPN decides to televise Washington versus St. Joe's because it's such a great matchup!

Judy, one of Nina's friends, laughs.

"St. Joe's is the number one team in the state," Judy says. "Skylar would need to score 40 points to beat them. No chance that'll happen. Thanks for embarrassing our school on national television!"

Skylar does not dignify Judy or Nina's doubts with an answer. She reflects on Mom's rule of not letting anyone else control her emotions. And Daddymoe said not to let the haters slow her down.

Besides, Skylar is not intimidated by St. Joe's.

The day of the big game, there's a noticeable buzz at Washington High School. ESPN arrives shortly after the morning bell to set up its wires and cameras. Teachers learn that a reporter for Sports Illustrated and several college coaches will be in attendance.

When they finally step on the court, the Panthers are blown away; the stands are full and fans line up along every wall of the gym! Coach McGraw is on one side of the gym, and Tennessee head coach Pat Summitt is on the other side.

The gym is very hot with all the people inside.

And like the temperature, the two teams start the game hot. They trade basket after basket, with Skylar pacing the Panthers. She scores 16 points in the first quarter!

But she's not done.

Skylar pours it on, aggressively driving toward the basket and dizzying St. Joe's with her crafty layups and floaters. On defense, Skylar and Em take turns chasing Melissa and denying the senior guard open looks at the basket.

In the second half, the Panthers jump out to a 10-point lead, but St. Joe's cuts the lead to five with five minutes left in the game.

Then Skylar ends any hopes of a St. Joe's comeback. She drills a corner three-pointer, steals the ball near midcourt, and drives hard to the basket.

And one!

While a St. Joe's player fouls her, Skylar makes the layup, earning a free throw, which she also makes.

St. Joe's misses a three-pointer on the next possession, and Skylar finds Ashley for an easy layup. St. Joe's cannot do much with their final few possessions, and the Panthers win 82–70.

Skylar finishes with 43 points!

A few days later, Skylar hears a knock at the front door.

Daddymoe opens the door and sees the mailman.

"How can I help you, Mr. Peterson?" Daddymoe says.

"I know you have a mailbox," Mr. Peterson says, "but I can't fit all of this in there."

He lifts up a large, plastic *Post Office* bin and shows Daddymoe.

"What's all that?" Daddymoe asks.

"I can't say for sure," Mr. Peterson says, "but

I'm guessing it's for your daughter."

Daddymoe grabs the bin, walks to the living room and dumps its contents on the floor. Daddymoe, Mom, and Skylar sift through it.

In all, there are 120 letters from 100 different colleges. They are *all* interested in Skylar!

McGraw and Pat Summitt were at the St. Joe's game, but many other coaches watched on ESPN. Skylar's 43 points against St. Joe's confirms all her middle school and AAU success.

The attention flatters Skylar, but she responds in the only way that makes sense to her—she heads to the backyard to work on her game.

The season breezes by, with the Panthers reaching the Class 4A State Championship game. The Panthers are underdogs no more. In fact, they are the top-ranked team in the state, and they are favored against unranked Castle High School.

Can the Panthers win the school's first basketball state title?

The Panthers play well against the Knights, scoring lots of points. But the Panthers' defense struggles, as Castle has four players in double figures, which means they each score at least 10 points. The Knights also make 50 percent of all their shots—a very high shooting percentage.

Skylar scores 22 points, including a state-record–tying four three pointers, and she blocks a game-high three shots. But the Panthers don't shoot as well as the Knights and lose 83–72.

Skylar exchanges handshakes with the Knights. She then heads to the end of the bench and sits down. She buries her head in her lap and cries.

Mom walks down to the court. She does not say anything but lovingly strokes Skylar's shoulder.

Knights coach Wayne Allen says in his press conference afterwards that he is thankful he does not have to face Skylar often.

"Skylar is a very special player," he says. "She is the type of player that will be good for many years to come."

As soon as she gets home, Skylar breaks down the film of the championship game for an hour then heads to her backyard court for another hour.

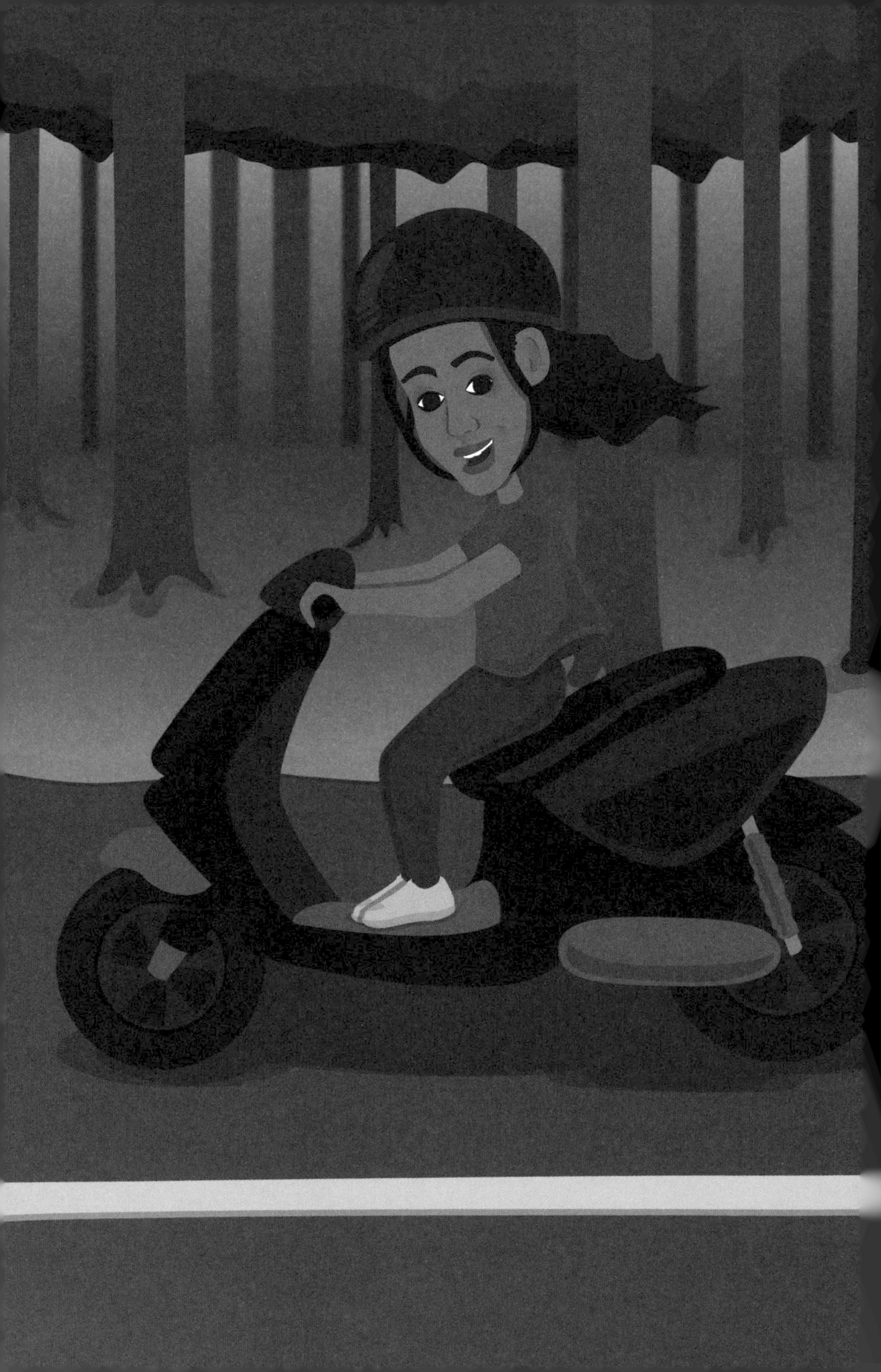

Chapter 26

Crash Course

At lunch during school, Skylar discovers that some classmates get a reward for good grades. At dinner, Skylar asks Daddymoe and Mom why she doesn't get anything.

"We don't ask you to do well in school," Mom says firmly. "We *expect* you to do well."

Daddymoe laughs. "Hypothetically speaking, what would you want for all As?"

Skylar hoped they would ask this.

"A few kids at school have mopeds," she says. "That would be *really* cool."

The next morning, Daddymoe and Mom call Skylar into the kitchen.

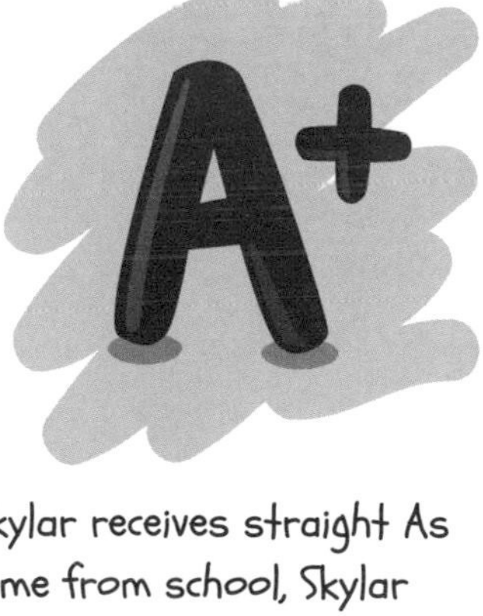
A+

"We discussed your request," Daddymoe says, "and we've decided you can earn a moped if you get straight As this semester."

Skylar jumps up and hugs Daddymoe and Mom.

Two months pass and, as planned, Skylar receives straight As on her report card. When she comes home from school, Skylar sees a moped with a red bow in the driveway. She claps and runs to inspect her new ride.

Daddymoe and Mom come outside and hand her the keys.

"Now let's set some ground rules," Mom says. "You ride this

RULES

to school, the King Center, or home. All those routes have nice, wide roads where you can ride safely. Nowhere else. Are we clear?"

Skylar nods.

Daddymoe takes Skylar to register her moped and apply for a special license that makes her a legal driver. Because she's under 18 years old, Skylar must wear goggles and a helmet at all times. Also, state law says mopeds cannot travel faster than 30 miles per hour. But Mom says Skylar's moped cannot travel faster than 20 miles per hour.

Safety first!

When they get home, Skylar calls Papa John.

"Can you come over?" Skylar asks her grandfather. "I got a moped, and I want to take you for a spin!"

Papa John drives over, and he briskly walks toward Skylar and her moped.

"Wow, look at that!" he says. "Let's go for a ride!"

Skylar grabs the handlebar, and Papa John sits behind her. They take off down the street, riding a few blocks, then turning around and going home.

"Dad, you don't have a helmet on," Mom says to Papa John. "I can't believe you did that!"

Papa John smiles.

"That's my Sky Pooh," he says, referring to Skylar by a special nickname only he calls her. "She wouldn't hurt her Papa."

For a few months, Skylar drives her moped to school in the morning, to the King Center in the afternoon, and back home before dark. But after school on a Thursday, Skylar arrives at the King Center and discovers that she cannot play basketball that day. Daddymoe is leading a special training session and the gym is closed.

Skylar sees Ashley, who delivers a message.

"Glad I ran into you," Ashley says. "Em invited us over to her house since we can't play. I wish I could, but my mom is on her way to pick me up, and we have to go run some errands. You should go, though!"

Skylar thinks through the situation.

Em's house is not on the approved destination list for her to ride to on her moped. But Em's house is less than two miles from her house.

It's only a little out of the way, Skylar thinks. *It's no big deal.*

She straps on her helmet, and heads for her moped. She carefully pulls out of the King Center parking lot and heads toward Em's house. The first mile is no problem, smooth sailing.

But just a few blocks from Em's house, Skylar must travel on a side road that is not paved. It's made of gravel, which is a mixture of rock fragments. Skylar gets nervous. The moped seems less stable traveling on the gravel. Skylar slows down.

But as she steers to the right, she loses control of the moped. It spins and slides, and her grip loosens. She tumbles onto the gravel and slams her head on the ground. Fortunately, her helmet protects her head!

Skylar quickly checks herself. *Whew! I'm in one piece,* she thinks. She takes off her helmet—and it falls apart. It split into two pieces!

Em hears the commotion, and she comes rushing toward the accident with her mother.

"Are you all right? Are you all right?" Emily yells.

"I'm fine," Skylar says, her voice quivering.

Em's mother checks Skylar and sees a tear in her top and scratches on her leg, just above her shoe line. Skylar says her left calf hurts.

"No serious damage," Em's mother says. "You are a lucky girl. Let me call your mom and let her know what happened."

After 20 minutes, Daddymoe and Mom arrive at Em's house.

"Skylar, what happened?" Mom says, concerned. "Are you OK?"

Mom inspects Skylar, as Skylar thinks of what to say. *Do I tell the truth, or make something up?*

But Mom looks like she already knows what is going through Skylar's mind.

Mom's Rule

"Remember, the worst thing to do is lie," Mom says. "If you're honest, your consequences will be less severe."

THE MIDDLE SCHOOL RULES OF SKYLAR DIGGINS

FLASHBACK

Honesty has always been Skylar's policy. Sometimes, she is too honest! When she is eight, Skylar watches a cartoon on television.

"Skylar, please go clean your room!" Mom says from the kitchen.

Skylar sighs. She does not want to clean her room. She wants to keep watching her cartoon. But she gets up, and she heads to the kitchen.

"Mom, when you told me to clean my room, I was thinking in my head that I didn't want to," Skylar says. "I'm sorry for thinking that."

Would Skylar make the right decision and tell Mom and Daddymoe the truth?

She takes a deep breath.

"I know I'm not supposed to ride my moped to Em's house," Skylar says, dropping her head. "I did not follow your rules, and I have no excuse."

Daddymoe and Mom are not pleased that Skylar did not obey them. But they are relieved that she's not badly hurt, and they are proud that she told the truth.

They have mercy on Skylar: She can no longer ride the moped, and she's grounded for a month. If she had lied, though, the punishment would have been much worse!

Skylar is sad that she cannot ride her moped anymore, but she accepts responsibility for her poor choice.

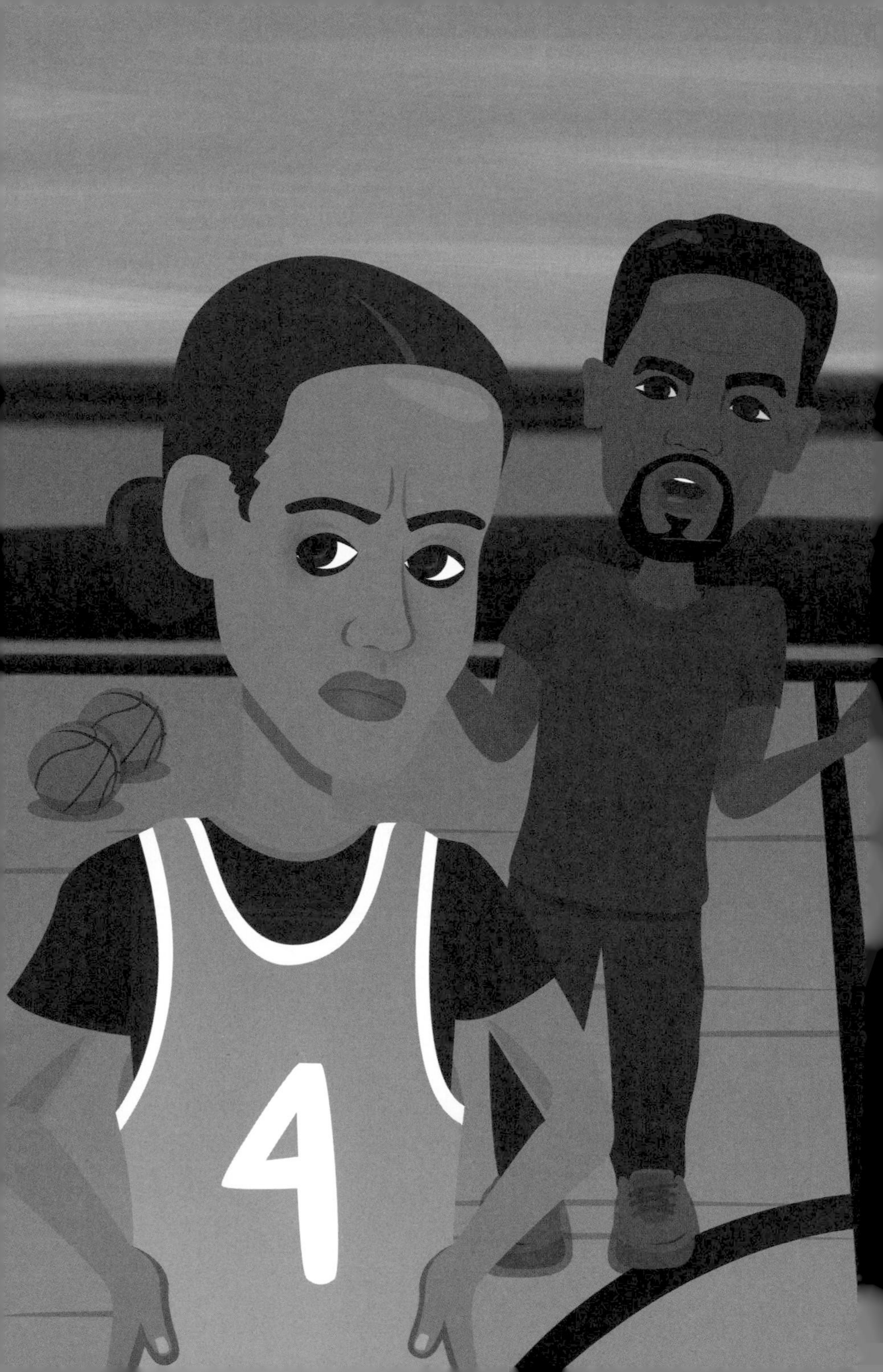

Chapter 27

Clashing with Daddymoe

When she is young, Skylar does not like to share Daddymoe. But as she matures, she realizes that some of her teammates *need* Daddymoe.

The Lady Soldiers call him Uncle Moe, and he helps each of them grow. On the court, he encourages Em to develop her basketball skills—and her confidence—and pushes Ashley to become more physical in the post. Off the court, he provides rides, assists with homework, and sets up "Girl Chats," inviting special guests who speak to them about topics like hygiene, image, and how they dress. Daddymoe wants his girls to be well-rounded.

Daddymoe is firm but fair with them.

Except for Skylar. She *feels* Daddymoe is too tough on her.

In one practice, Em aims a pass way above Shearice's head and the ball sails out of bounds.

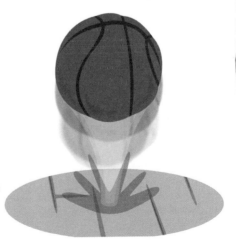

"It's all right, Em," Daddymoe says, clapping his hands. "Make a play on defense."

On the next possession, Skylar throws a pass too soft into the post for Ashley, and the defender intercepts the ball.

"Come on, Skylar!" Daddymoe shouts. "Get your head in the game!"

Skylar growls under her breath.

Later on, Skylar goes for a steal and the offensive player scoots past and makes a layup.

"Where is the D? Where is the defense?" Daddymoe asks loudly. He subs Skylar out.

When practice ends, Skylar quickly collects her belongings and storms off toward the exit. She wants to walk home but it's dark out.

After five minutes, Daddymoe walks up to the car. He unlocks the doors, climbs into the driver's seat, and steers the car toward home. Skylar does not say a word.

When they pull into the driveway, Daddymoe turns to Skylar and asks, "You all right?"

Skylar erupts.

"Why are you so hard on me?" she blurts out. "It's not fair!"

Daddymoe exhales. His face softens.

Daddymoe's Rule

"Skylar, you have to hold yourself to your own standard," Daddymoe says. "You have to allow your elevator to go to the top floor. You owe it to yourself to see how good you can be."

Daddymoe adds that because he is a coach, he does not want the other girls—especially the few who do not have fathers—to feel like he treats Skylar better than them.

Skylar can understand that.

After talking for 15 minutes, the two get out of the car and hug. Skylar loves her Daddymoe.

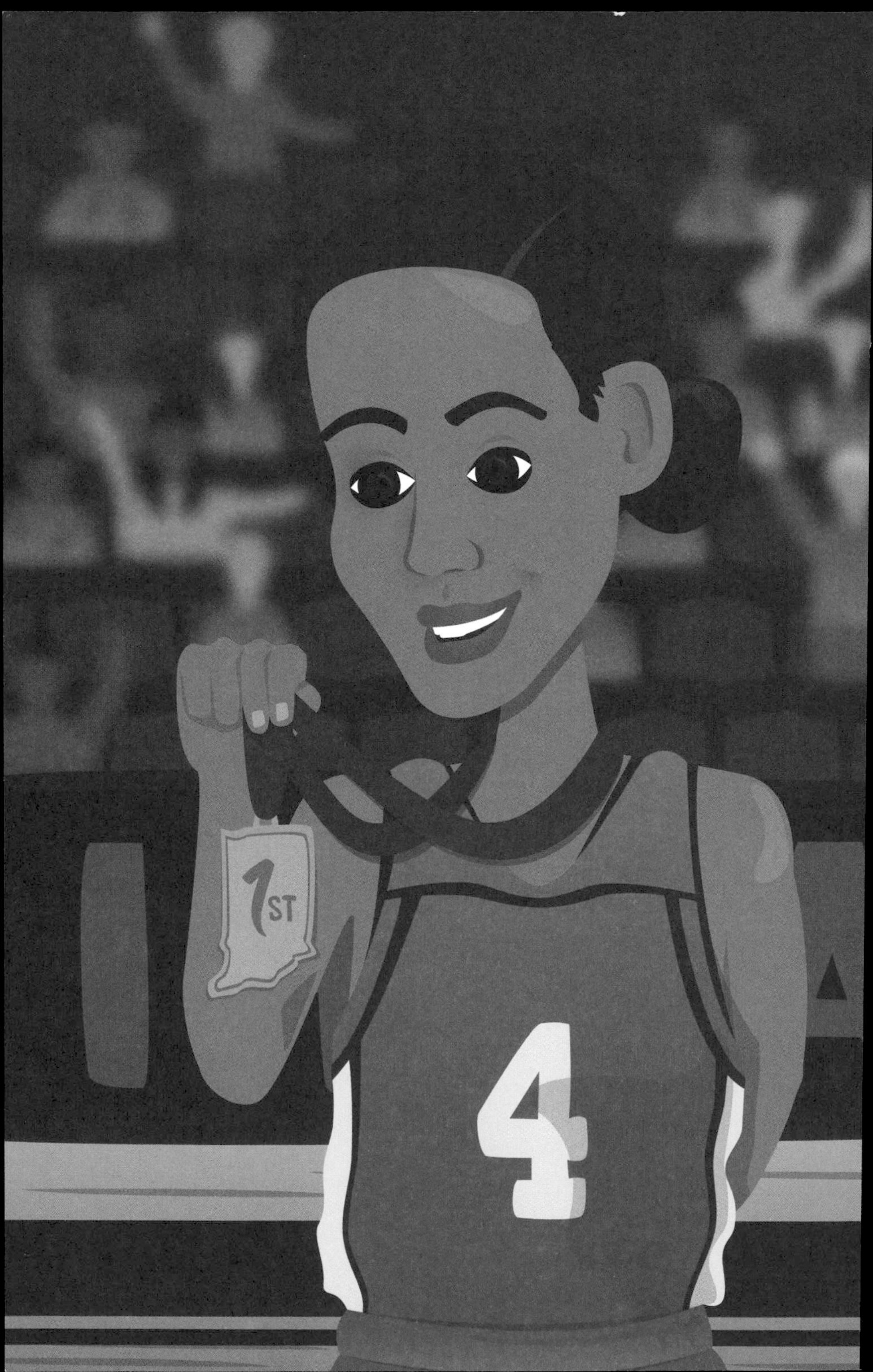
1ST
4

Chapter 28

Stepping Up

After losing the state championship, the Panthers return all five of their starters. But this is Ashley's senior year.

Because they have been playing together for so many years, Ashley, Em, and Skylar get very intense with one another. During a practice, Skylar makes a routine pass to Ashley. But the defender slides in front of Ashley and steals the ball.

"Catch the ball!" Skylar yells.

"Well, give me a better pass next time!" Ashley replies.

Skylar's expectations of herself, however, are higher than ever. If she misses even one shot, she insists on running the play again. When practice is over, she refuses to leave the court until she makes 150 shots, no matter how long that takes her.

Before the first game, two teammates get into a screaming match with two other girls near the principal's office.

The principal hears the ruckus and rushes into the hallway.

"What's going on here?" he asks.

Skylar's teammates continue to yell and point at the other girls. They are arguing over a boy.

"Now stop right there," the principal says. "If you lay your hands on anyone, you will be suspended!"

The other girls try to get the final word in, which offends one of Skylar's teammates. Although the principal is standing between them, the two sets of girls press forward and exchange shoves.

The principal immediately separates them with the help of two other teachers, who sprint from their classrooms.

"That's it!" the principal says. "All four of you are suspended! Take them all to the office right now!"

The next day, the Panthers play their first game of the season without the two players. They are sorely missed, since they are both excellent defenders.

South Side High School from Fort Wayne score easily, and they beat the Panthers 78–72. Though favored to win the state title, the Panthers lose their first game of the season.

Before their next practice, Skylar calls everyone together. She is a sophomore, and usually juniors and seniors lead high school teams. But Skylar has something she *must* say.

Calmly, she looks directly at her suspended teammates first then scans the faces of everyone else.

"It's got to be about *we*, not about *me*," Skylar says. "The decisions you make don't just affect you. They affect this team. If we're going to achieve our goal, we have to be unselfish and put the team above everything else."

Everyone nods, even the suspended teammates.

Despite her age, Skylar becomes a leader for the Panthers.

She tells teammates they need to assume more of a business approach on game days. At Washington High School, students have to wear uniforms, but the Panthers get to wear their warmup suits on game days. To make everyone look even fancier, Skylar offers to paint anyone's fingernails during lunchtime. Skylar prefers to paint her own nails the color of the other team!

In the locker room, Skylar is particular about her hair, styling it in different ways, depending on her mood. When she walks to the court, she wants to display her beauty. On the court, she wants to display her inner beast.

Skylar plays with a rare intensity, slapping the floor to fire up teammates and blanketing opponents with her defense. She sometimes celebrates big shots or key passes with an emphatic fist pump.

Though not always the fastest player, Skylar is relentless and plays at a speed opponents just cannot keep up with. She averages nearly five steals per game, which is a lot!

The Panthers win by an average 25.3 points per game. They return to the championship game and are favored against Columbus East.

Can the Panthers pull it off *this* time?

The Panthers start strong, with Skylar blocking an early shot and stealing a pass. Ashley scores four points, as the Panthers jump out to a 7–0 lead.

But Columbus East rallies and ties the game at 16 points after the first quarter. In the second quarter, the Panthers outscore Columbus East 20–6, with Skylar scoring nine points.

The Panthers score 30 points in the third quarter, with Skylar draining 13 of them. They win the game 84–64. Skylar leads all players with 27 points, but she also grabs 17 rebounds!

Skylar, Em, and Ashley

share a group hug. They win AAU titles together, but they also wanted to lead Washington High School to its first basketball championship.

They did it!

What makes the championship even more special is that all of Skylar's loved ones attend the game then celebrate afterwards at Granny Stella's.

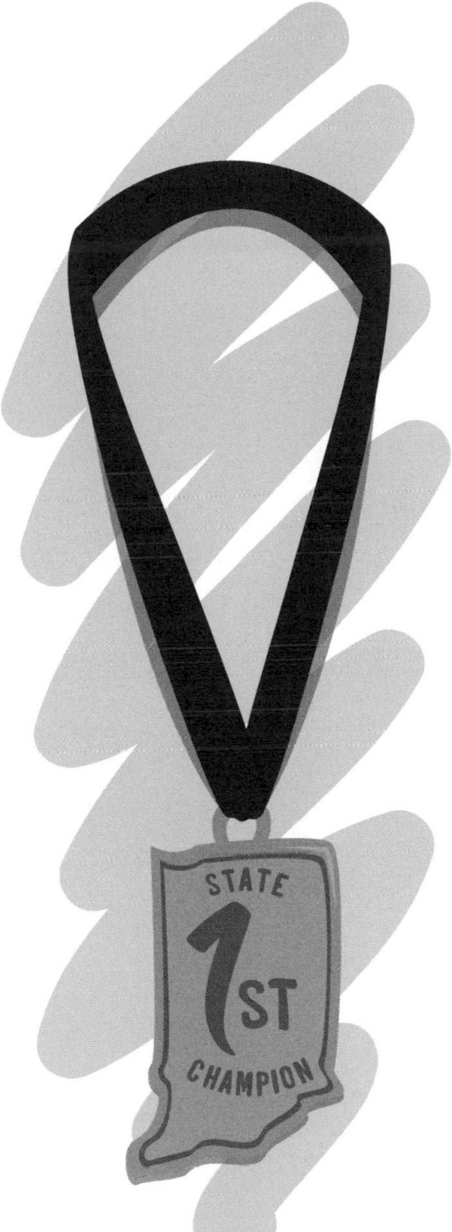
STATE
1ST
CHAMPION

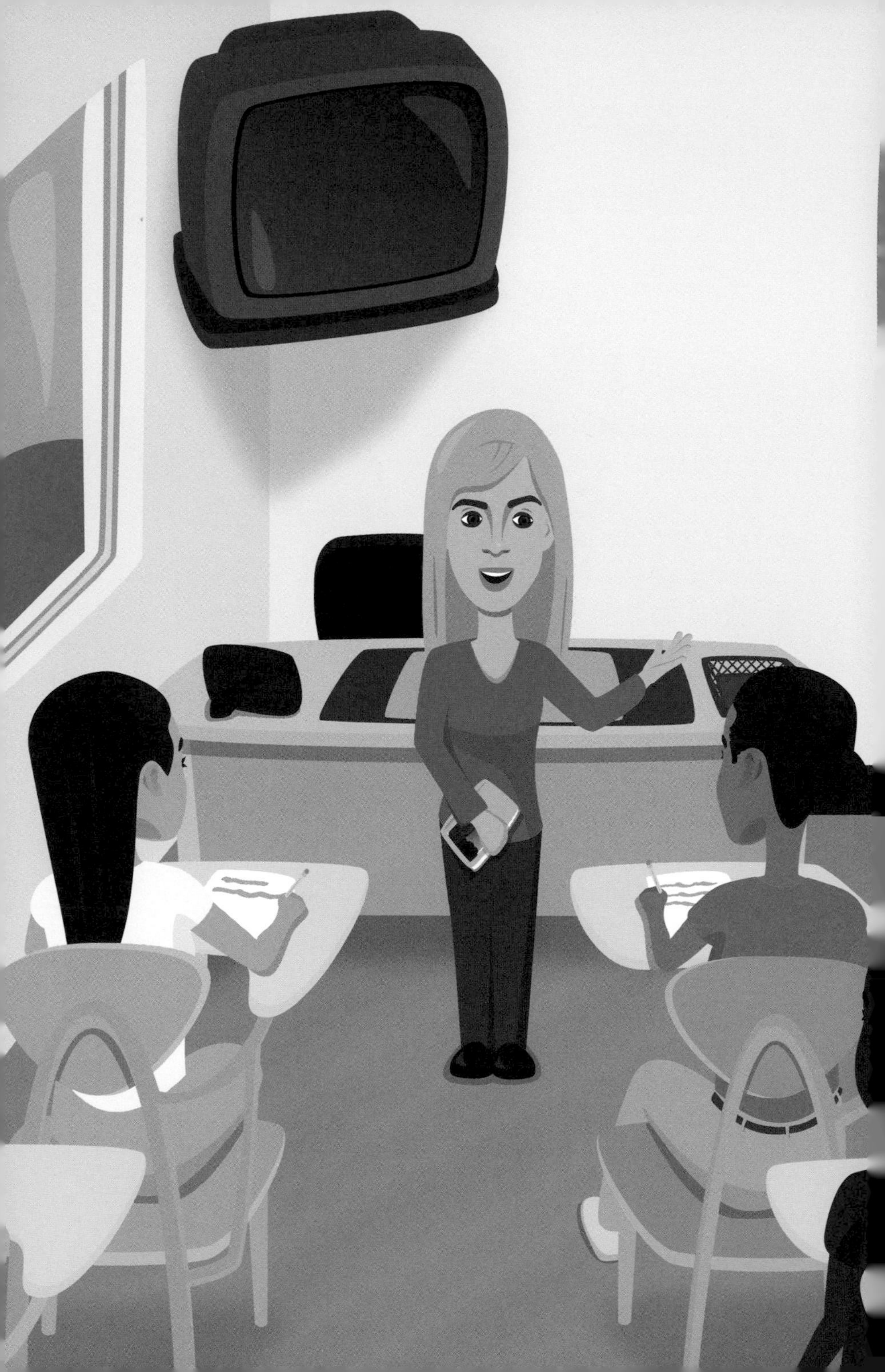

Chapter 29

Ms. Ehmer

After the state title, Skylar starts to feel lots of pressure about her future. The bins of mail continue to come from colleges, and people always ask her where she is going to play college basketball.

"I don't know," Skylar says for what seems to be the millionth time. "It's a big decision, and I want to take my time."

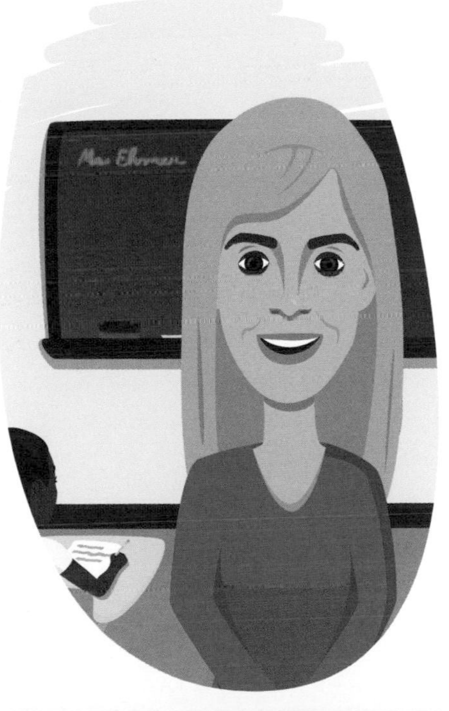

Skylar does not want to complain about her good fortune. Most students do not get full scholarship offers from a college, let alone many scholarship offers from all parts of the country.

She talks to Daddy on the phone frequently, and Mom and Daddymoe are always supportive.

But one person at school she confides in is Mrs. Ehmer. As an English teacher, Mrs. Ehmer is creative and passionate, nudging her

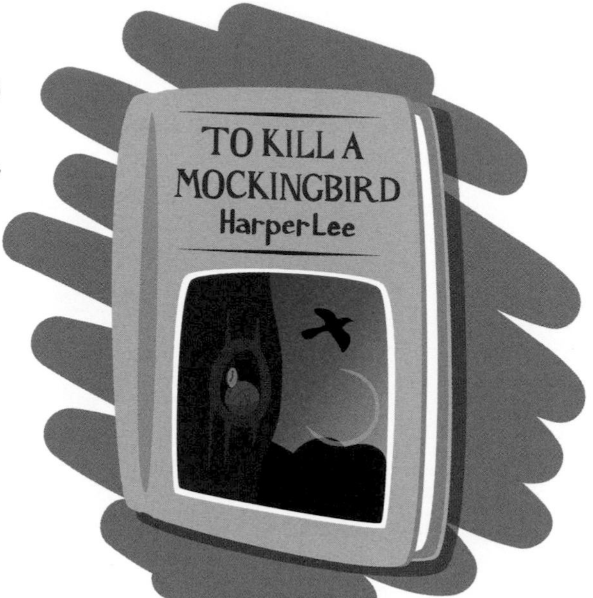
TO KILL A MOCKINGBIRD
Harper Lee

students to read challenging books and write inspiring papers.

That, however, isn't the only reason Skylar appreciates Mrs. Ehmer.

Like Mrs. Wilson, her choir teacher, Mrs. Ehmer listens more than she talks. Mrs. Ehmer has a calming presence about her. In Room 703, Mrs. Ehmer sits at her old, metal desk. During homeroom, Skylar often pulls up a salmon-colored student desk, and they freely speak, about basketball, about school, about life.

Mrs. Ehmer empathizes with all the stress young Skylar faces. Teammates, coaches, classmates, teachers, community leaders, all of them *expect* her to carry the Panthers to greatness.

Mrs. Ehmer's Rule

"Basketball does not define you," Mrs. Ehmer says to Skylar. "Even if you don't play anymore, I love you all the same. You're smart, you're kind, and you're a great kid."

An English teacher named Mr. F gets nominated as a "Memorable Teacher" every year by a dozen different students. Mr. F always sits at the largest table at the award banquet to receive his award in front of hundreds of people.

Mrs. Ehmer does not receive any nominations. That bothers Skylar. She believes Mrs. Ehmer is a teacher deserving of recognition. Skylar becomes the first student at Washington High School to recommend Mrs. Ehmer as a "Memorable Teacher." In the spring, while at home, Mrs. Ehmer receives an invitation.

She is invited to the awards banquet! She'll get to dress up, eat a nice dinner, and receive an award.

At school the next morning, Mrs. Ehmer approaches Skylar's locker.

"That was so thoughtful of you to nominate me," Mrs. Ehmer tells Skylar. "Thank you so, so much!"

At her table at the awards banquet, Mrs. Ehmer sits with her husband, Skylar, Mom, and Daddymoe. Skylar is delighted to see someone else recognized for their hard work.

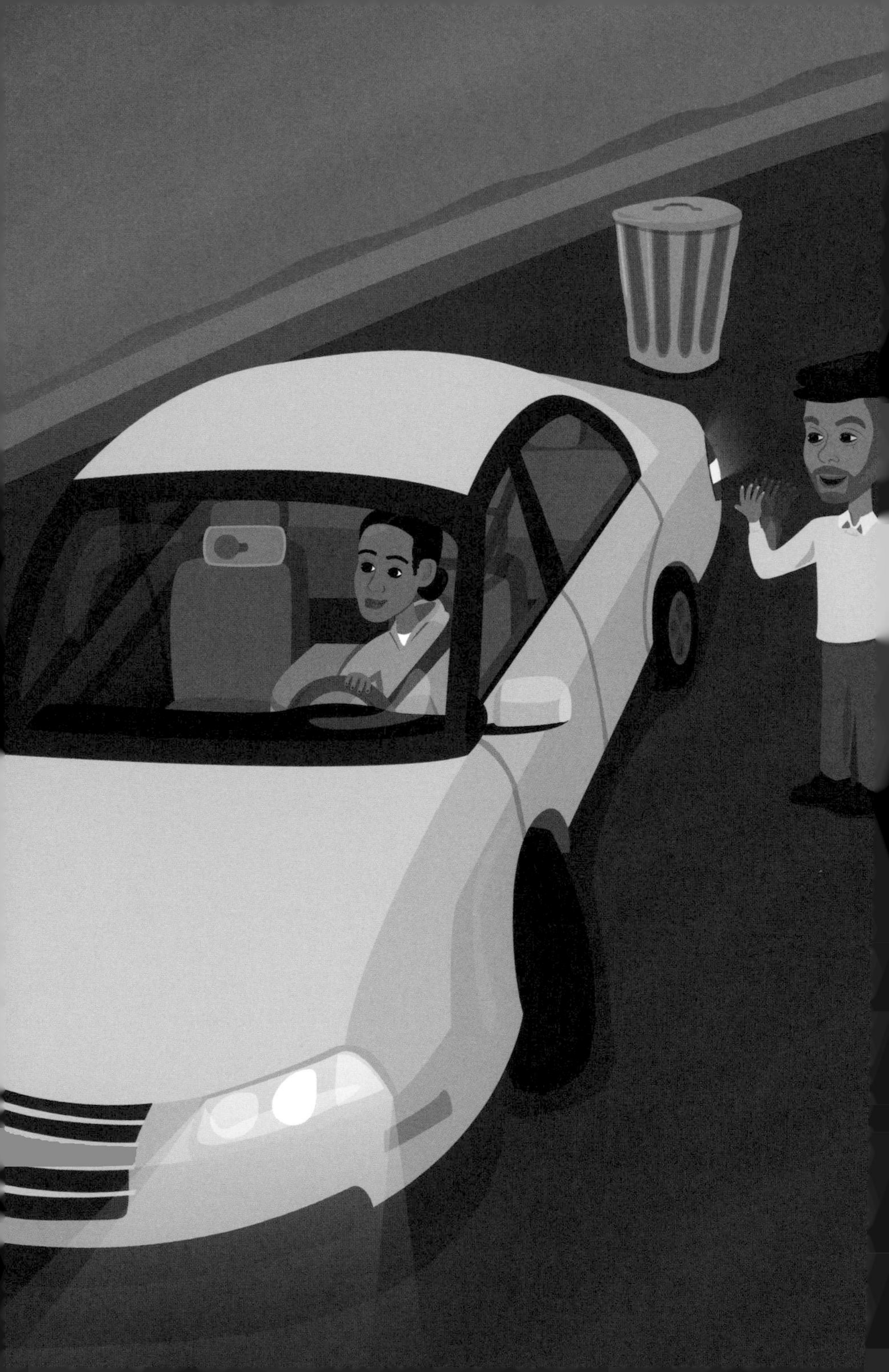

Chapter 30

Papa John

When she's still 15, Skylar practices driving with her learner's permit. But she wants to take her driver's test as soon as she turns 16!

Skylar is eager to drive a car. She wants the freedom she briefly enjoyed when she rode her moped. Behind the wheel of a car, Skylar is alert and careful, always abiding by the speed limit and staying in her assigned lane.

Except Skylar has one problem. She struggles to *parallel park*. That is when a driver parks his or her vehicle behind or in front of another car parallel to the curb. Parallel parking is one of the biggest challenges for many drivers, especially new ones.

Skylar takes Driver's Education, where she practices driving in a car with a teacher.

Many Driver's Ed cars are unusual. The passenger seat, where the driving teacher sits, also features a steering wheel, brake, and gas pedal. That allows the teacher to help the student driver.

Skylar excels in every other aspect of driving except parallel parking! On her first try, she leaves the car too far from the imaginary curb, and she knocks over an orange and white cone with her rear bumper.

"Come on!" the Driver's Ed teacher yells. "You would have smashed another car."

Skylar takes a deep breath and tries again. She eases the car into the spot, but she bumps into the orange and white cone with the front bumper.

"It's not that hard!" the teacher says. "Let me do this so I can get to my next appointment!"

Skylar sighs. She knows she will need to master parallel parking if she is going to pass her driver's test. She knows exactly who to ask for help!

She remembers that Papa John taught her mom how to drive. Besides, Papa John is an excellent driver, often taking Skylar to and from practices.

"Papa John," Skylar says on the phone. "Can you help me with parallel parking?"

"Of course, Sky Pooh!" Papa John says. "I'll come get you Sunday afternoon, and we can practice."

Papa John picks up Skylar on Sunday, and he returns to his neighborhood, where there is not much traffic. Papa John has

already lined up garbage cans near the curb on the side of his house.

"Skylar, I want you to drive around the block and park my car in that spot," Papa John says, pointing to a space. Skylar listens to Papa John. When she returns, she

triggers the turn signals then backs Papa John's gray car into the space. Her rear bumper hits a garbage can.

"Why can't I do this?" Skylar says, frustrated.

Papa John's Rule

"You can learn from history, but you cannot dwell on history," Papa John tells Skylar. "It's what you do next that matters, baby girl!"

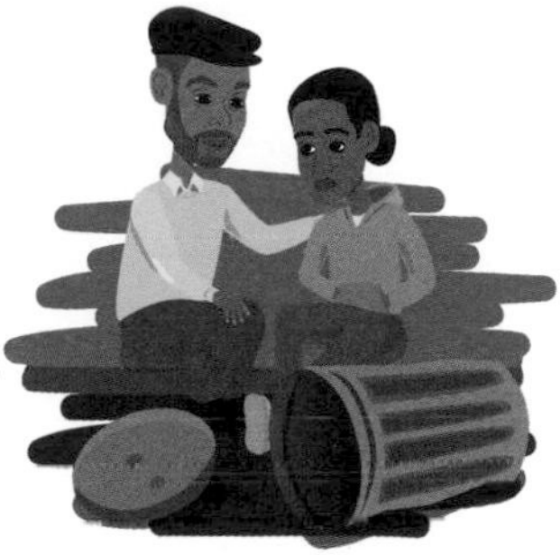

"Make sure you look out the side and rear view mirrors," Papa John says. "Circle around the block and try again!"

Skylar drives around and prepares to park. She backs into the space, turns the steering wheel and parks the car.

"How is that?" Skylar proudly asks.

"That was much better," Papa John says. "But you're about a foot-and-a-half from the curb. You could get a ticket if you're more than a foot from the curb so let's try one more time. You've got this next one!"

Skylar grips the steering wheel, takes a breath, and drives around the block again.

She puts the car in reverse and backs into the spot, looking intently at her side and rearview mirrors. Then she shifts the car into drive, turns the wheel toward the curb and inches the car forward. She puts the car into park and waits to hear from Papa John.

"That's perfect, baby girl!" Papa John says. "Now do it again!"

Skylar perfectly parallel parks the car three more times. She feels confident now.

"You did a great job!" Papa John says. "You should be able to pass that test with no problem."

"Thanks, Papa!" Skylar says.

Two weeks later, Skylar aces her driver's test.

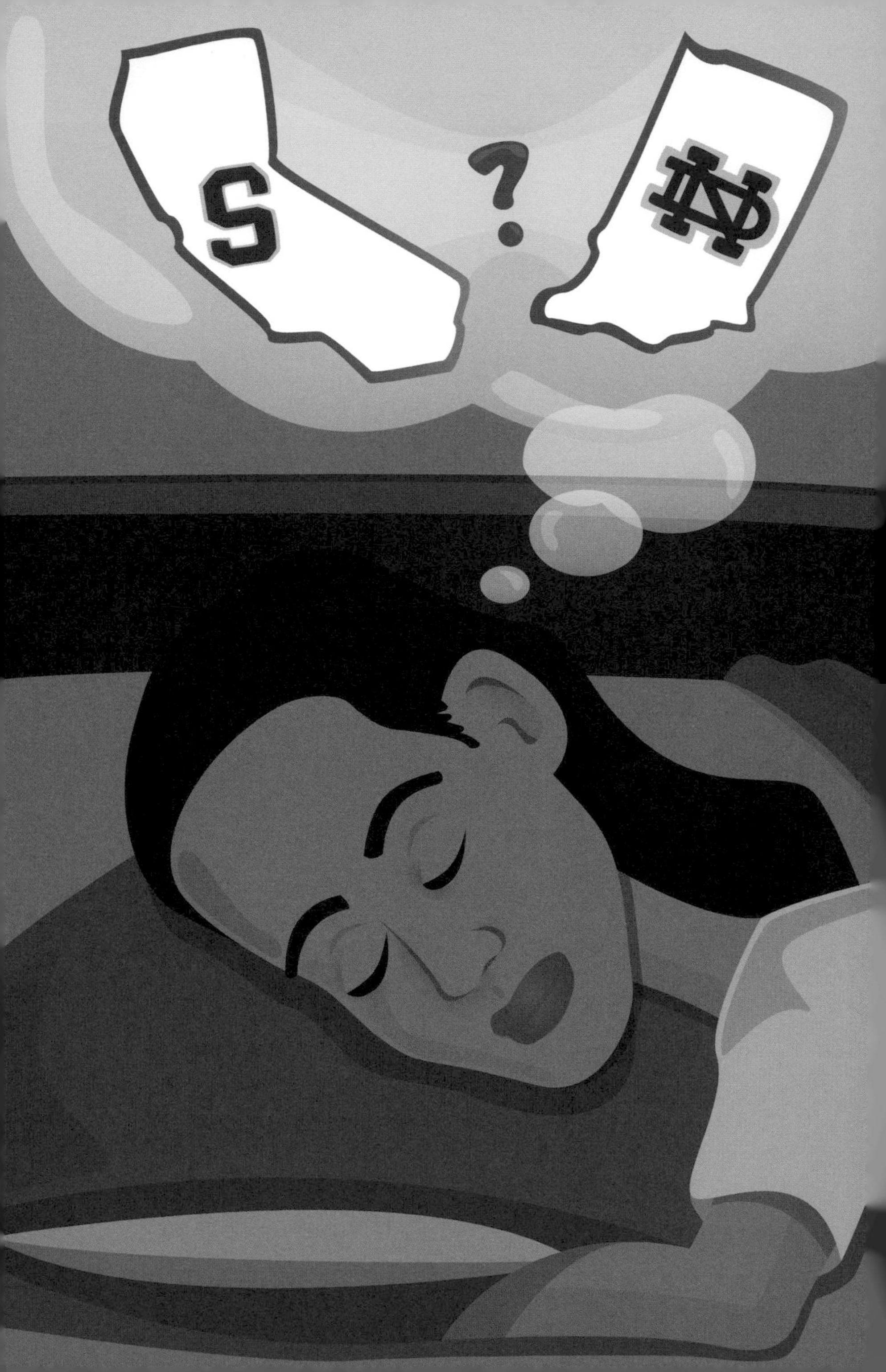

Chapter 31

The Decision

The Panthers basketball team is not expected to go to the state title game again. Four seniors, including Ashley, have left for college. The team is young, and Skylar needs to do more of everything: Score, shoot, and rebound.

Skylar rises to the challenge, making 50 percent of her shots and leading the state with an average of 29.5 points per game. She also averages 7.6 rebounds, 4.5 assists, and 3.9 steals per game.

She does all this despite being double- and triple-teamed by opposing defenders.

The Panthers defy the odds and reach the state championship game again, but they lose to Carmel High School, 84–72.

During the spring and summer, everywhere she goes, Skylar gets asked where she plans to go to college.

"I don't know," Skylar repeatedly says. "I haven't made a decision."

In the fall of her senior year, Skylar makes a big decision. She will pick her college *before* her senior basketball season starts. That way, she can enjoy her final high school season.

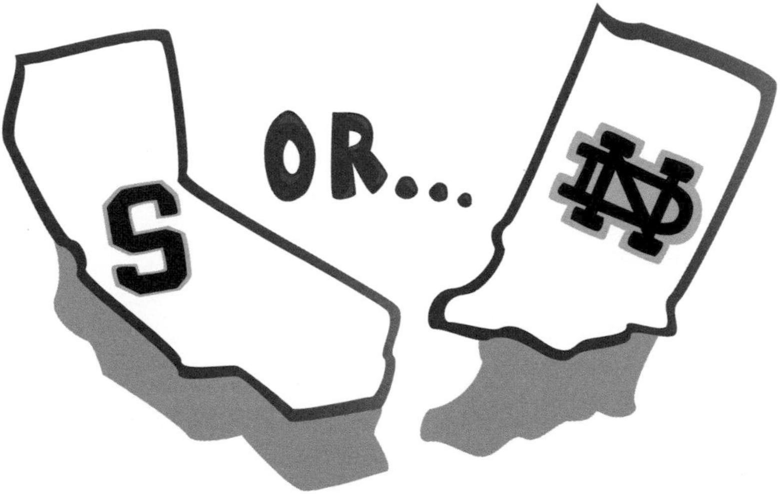
S
OR...
ND

Though every major college program offers her a scholarship, Skylar narrows her list to three schools: Stanford, Notre Dame, and Penn State. She likes Stanford because it represents a new adventure, since it's over 2,000 miles away from South Bend, and the Cardinal make deep runs in the NCAA Tournament. She likes Notre Dame because her family can watch her games. And she likes Penn State because Em plays there and Coquese Washington coaches there.

On Tuesday, November 18, Skylar spends two hours speaking to Mom, Daddy, and Daddymoe about her options. She appreciates that all of them want her to make her own decision.

"Mom, I'm ready," Skylar says at 10 p.m. "I'm going to call Stanford coach VanDerveer with my decision to go there."

"Skylar, it's really late," Mom says. "You should sleep on it.

Then you'll know the right decision in the morning."

As usual, Skylar listens to her mom's advice. The next day, she *feels* different.

She *wants* to play at Notre Dame, where she can play in front of her family and help the Fighting Irish become an elite program. Though they won the national title in 2001, since then the Fighting Irish have not advanced past the Sweet 16 in the NCAA Tournament. The Sweet 16 is the round that means only 16 teams are left to contend for the championship.

After school on November 19, Skylar calls Coach VanDerveer and Coach Washington to let them know she will not be attending their respective schools. Then Skylar, Daddymoe, Mom, and Junior drive to the Joyce Center, where Notre Dame plays Evansville.

Coach McGraw and Niele Ivey, now an assistant at Notre Dame, see Skylar and her family before tipoff. The coaches are nervous.

"Why is she here?" Coach Ivey asks Coach McGraw. "I hope she's not here to tell us no. That would be cold."

Notre Dame blows out Evansville 96–61, and Skylar and her family walk toward the locker room. Skylar grabs a stat sheet and approaches Coach McGraw and Coach Ivey.

"Man, you have a lot of guards," Skylar says. "Where are you going to fit me in?"

Coach McGraw and Coach Ivey exchange puzzled looks.

"What?" Coach McGraw asks.

Skylar smiles.

She's committing to Notre Dame!

The next morning, Skylar makes it official, signing her National Letter of Intent. Within hours, the women's basketball program sells 1,500 more season tickets.

"There are some kids in the recruiting process that you feel like you have to get for the future of your program," Coach McGraw says. "Skylar was in our own backyard. We couldn't let her get away!"

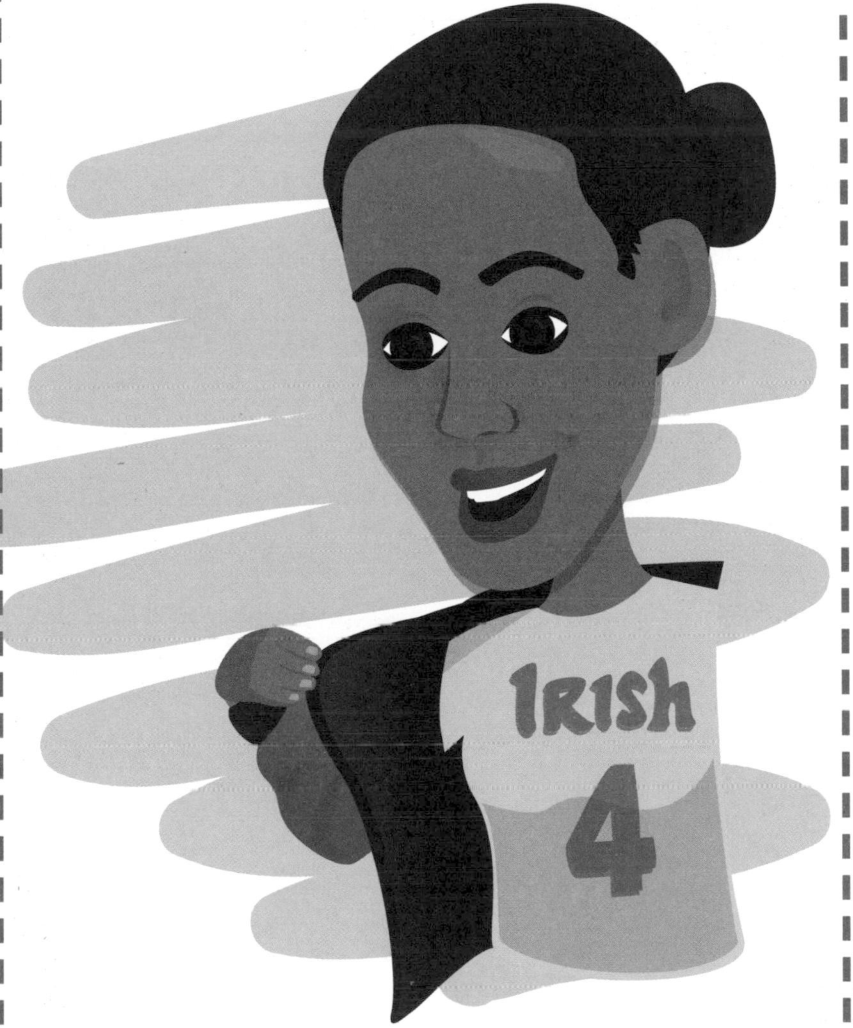
IRISH
4

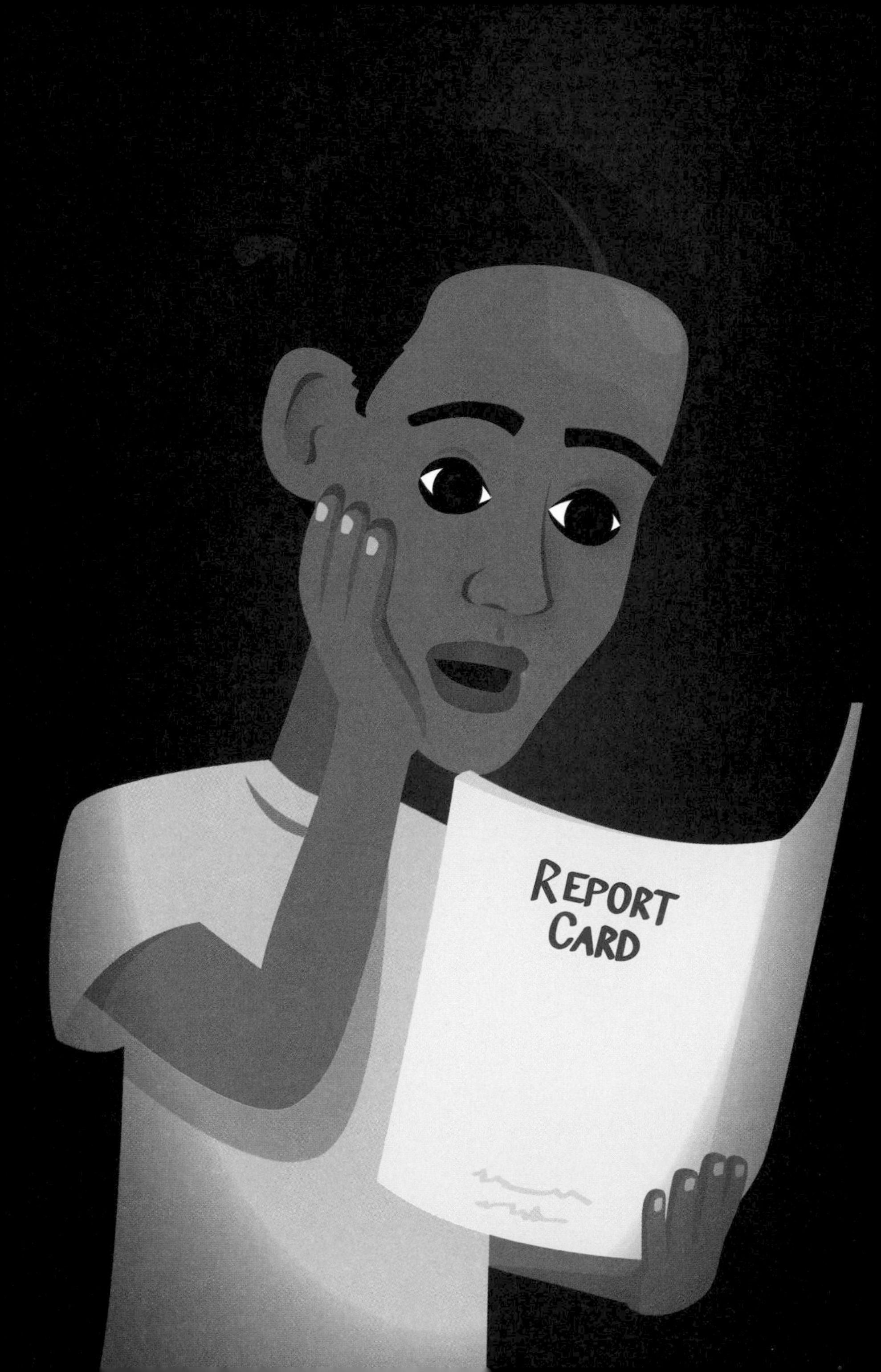
REPORT CARD

Chapter 32

Unfair B

Skylar is thankful that she has a scholarship to a great school like Notre Dame. But she still has an academic goal she set *before* high school: to graduate with a perfect 4.0 grade point average.

Skylar wants to honor her parents, who instill in her the importance of being a *scholar* athlete. Besides, she knows she cannot play basketball forever!

In her freshman, sophomore, and junior years of high school, Skylar earned perfect marks in all her classes. But during her senior year, she deals with a complicated problem.

After Skylar and her classmates turn in a 10-page history paper, Mr. Fuller leaves school early

because of a family emergency. He rushes to the airport, where he flies to his hometown of Nashville, Tennessee. His mother is very sick.

The following week, Mr. Fuller returns the 10-page papers in class, except Skylar does not get one.

"Where is my paper?" Skylar asks.

Mr. Fuller shrugs.

"You never turned one in," he tells Skylar.

A puzzled look sweeps across Skylar's face.

"I *definitely* turned one in, Mr. Fuller," Skylar respectfully says. "I *always* do my work."

Mr. Fuller nods.

"Let me look into it," he says.

Skylar does not worry.

But the next week, Mr. Fuller asks Skylar to stick around after class.

"I don't know how to tell you this," Mr. Fuller says. "But I investigated everything, and I couldn't find your paper. Just print out another copy."

Skylar usually writes papers on the family's computer at home. But Daddymoe was using the computer the week before the history paper was due, so she wrote it at a school computer lab.

"I'll go check with Mrs. Bryant in the computer lab," Skylar says. "I remember which computer I was on."

"Bring me the paper," Mr. Fuller says, "and we should be fine."

Skylar jogs to the computer lab. She wants to get all this sorted out right away! She returns to the computer she used and searches through all the folders on it. She cannot find her name.

"Mrs. Bryant, can you help me, please?" Skylar asks.

When Mrs. Bryant walks over, Skylar tells her about the

missing history paper and asks if she can figure out a way to track it down.

"Oh no, Skylar," Mrs. Bryant says. "I'm afraid we won't be able to help you. We delete all the files off each computer at the end of every week."

Skylar's heart races. *What am I going to do?*

At home, Skylar tells Mom and Daddymoe everything.

"I'll call your teacher tomorrow morning," Mom says. "We'll get to the bottom of this."

But the next night at dinner, Skylar receives bad news from Mom.

"I talked to Mr. Fuller *and* Vice Principal Taylor, but they say there is nothing they can do since there is no paper," Mom says. "You will receive an incomplete on that assignment."

An incomplete is the same as an F—a letter grade Skylar has *never* gotten before. An F will mean she will not graduate with a 4.0 grade point average.

"Mom, this is wrong," Skylar protests. "I did that paper. I promise."

Daddymoe's Rule

"Control what *you* can control," Daddymoe says. "When you can't, don't worry or stress; move on. You know you did it, and you have to be OK with that."

At the end of the semester, Skylar tears open the envelope containing her report card.

Maybe—just maybe—they figured out the history paper.

But when she looks at the report card, Skylar sees a letter she's never received before: B. Given all the assignments in History,

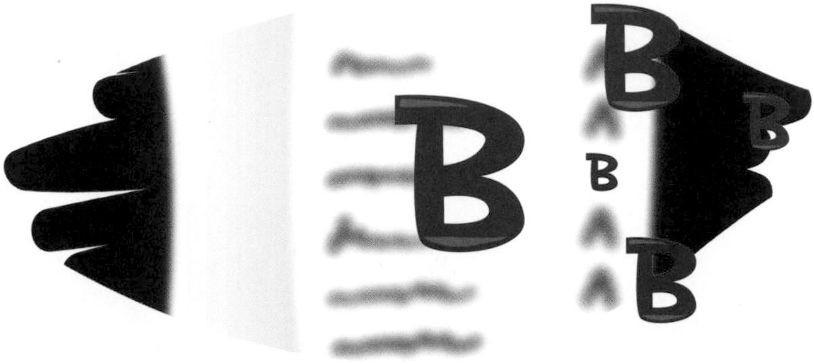
B
B
B
B
B

the F lowered her grade from an A to a B. Skylar is devastated but only for a few moments. She thinks about Daddymoe's words. *Control what you can control.*

She cannot control that her paper went missing, or that school administrators gave her an F anyway. What she can control, she decides, is to save all her work, double check all her assignments, and make sure she gets As on the rest of her high school classes.

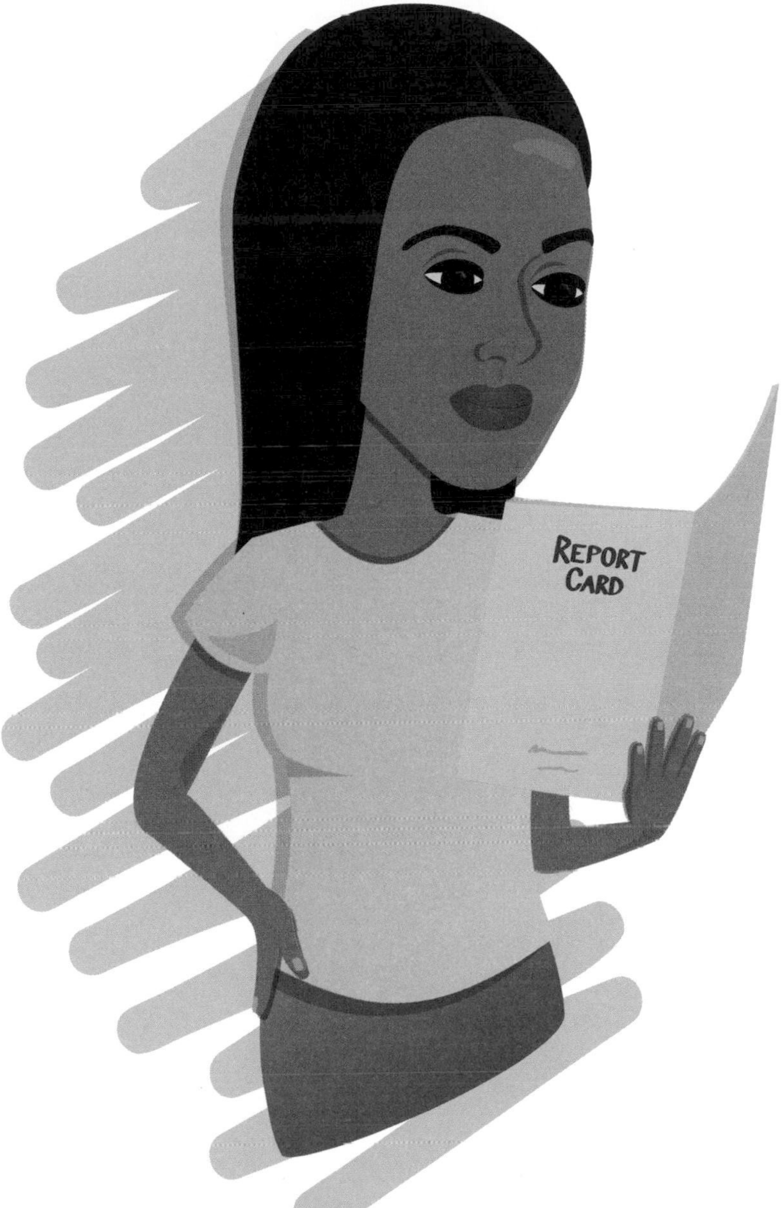
REPORT
CARD

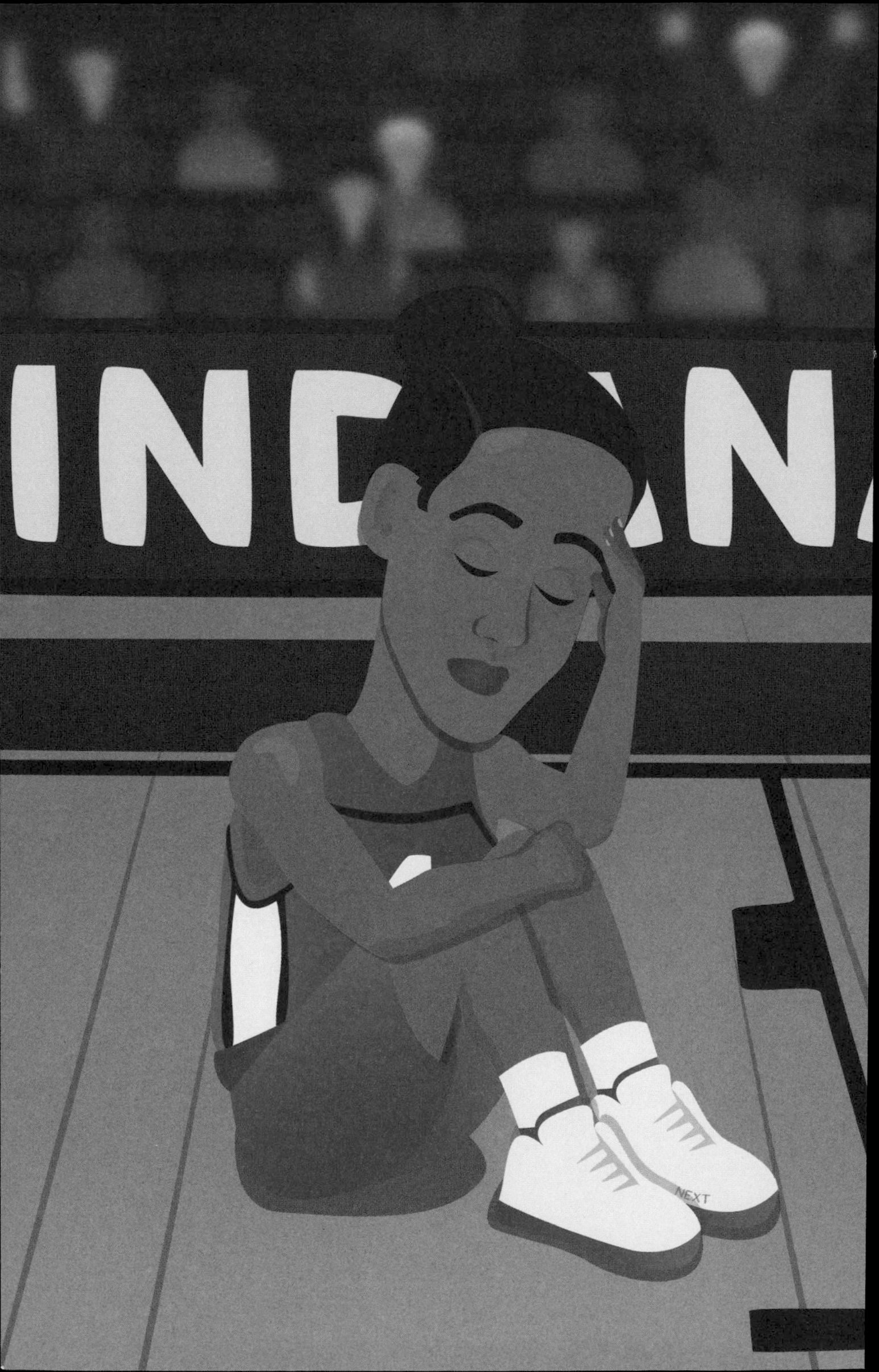
NEXT

Chapter 33

Senior Year

With her college decision made, Skylar focuses on her senior season with the Panthers. She wants to win another state title, especially since Daddymoe is now the head coach!

The expectations for the Panthers, however, is low. Skylar is once again the star, but the Panthers have a young, inexperienced team. Before the team's first official practice, Daddymoe calls Skylar into his office.

"There's good, there's great, and there's special," Daddymoe says to Skylar. "There are a lot of players who are good, and not as many are great. But very few are special."

Daddymoe's Rule

"How you become special is to help people become the best that *they* can be; help others tap into *their* greatness," Daddymoe says. "This season, I don't need you to be great. I need you to be special."

Skylar's heart beats fast. She thrives on challenges, and Daddymoe laid a great one before her.

"Are you up for it?" Daddymoe asks.

Skylar looks Daddymoe in the eyes and confidently says, "I am."

In the first six games, the Panthers average 88 points per game and allow just 30 points! During a Christmas tournament, the Panthers edge out a team from Newark, New Jersey, 75–73, and also defeat a team from Madison, Alabama.

Skylar plays brilliantly: she leads all players in the state with 29 points per game, and she averages 5.4 steals per game. She also shoots 55 percent from the field, which is a very, very high percentage for a guard.

Despite many questions about the strength of the team, the Panthers return to the state title game for a fourth consecutive year!

The opponent, though, is ranked the number one girls' basketball team in the entire country. Ben Davis High School is 29–0, and the school features seven players who would go on to play Division I college basketball. An eighth girl would run track at Indiana University.

Playing the Panthers, Ben Davis High School builds a 10-point halftime lead, and they lead by 11 points with less than three minutes remaining in the game.

Skylar refuses to quit.

In the final 100 seconds, Skylar scores eight points, including a layup that ties the game at 69 points!

A Ben Davis High School player makes a runner with 1.4 seconds left to give her team the lead again. Skylar attempts a desperation

shot past half court, but she misses.

Ben Davis High School wins.

Skylar's game-high 29 points are not enough.

Though she wants to cry, Skylar congratulates the players from Ben Davis High School, and encourages her teammates.

But she realizes something as she accepts the second-place medallion: this is her *final* high school basketball game.

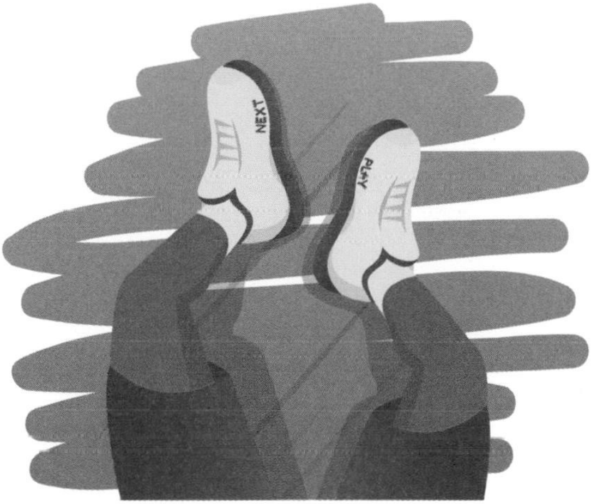
NEXT
PLAY

Tears trickle down Skylar's cheeks. She wishes she could have won one more title for her school, for her community, and for her Daddymoe.

Soon, Skylar sees dozens of family members walk toward her. One after another hugs Skylar and shares a message.

"Granny loves you," Granny Stella tells her.

"You never gave up," Papa John tells her. "You'll make the next one."

"You were amazing," Daddy whispers in her ear.

"You did your best," Mom says. "I couldn't be prouder."

"We didn't win," Daddymoe says, "but you were special because you made every teammate better. I love you."

The family celebrates with dinner at a local restaurant. Usually, Skylar would want to rush home and practice. But that night, Skylar relishes the time with all her loved ones.

Epilogue

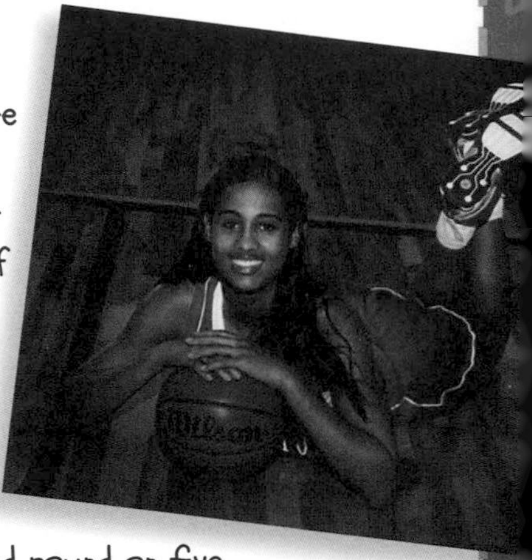

As a senior at Washington High School, Skylar wins every major state and national award: Indiana Miss Basketball, Gatorade National Player of the Year, and Gatorade Athlete of the Year.

Though they win the national title in 2001, the Fighting Irish do not advance deep into the NCAA Tournament over the next eight seasons, losing in the first or second round on five occasions.

Many expect Skylar to make Notre Dame an elite program again.

"The expectations she had for herself and those people put on her were hard to live up to," Coach McGraw says. "But she didn't just live up to them, she exceeded the expectations."

A four-time All-American, Skylar leads Notre Dame to three Final Fours, including two national championship games, and two Big East titles. Notre Dame was 0–20 against the University of Tennessee and 4–28 against the University of Connecticut before Skylar arrives on campus. During her four seasons, Notre Dame was undefeated against Tennessee, and Skylar leads the Fighting Irish to seven victories against Connecticut.

When she leaves Notre Dame, she shares no fewer than 32 game, season, and career records at the school. She also earns the distinction as one of just six NCAA Division I players to compile 2,000 points, 500 rebounds, 500 assists, and 300 steals in a career.

Off the court, Skylar earns her bachelor's degree in management-entrepreneurship. In fact, she's proud to have been a four-time Big East All-Academic Team selection.

None of it—the basketball accolades and records, nor the academic achievements—comes easily to Skylar.

"I had a tutor for every class at Notre Dame," Skylar says. "I had to ask a lot of questions. I had to work so hard."

Skylar applies that same work ethic on the court.

"I am not the fastest, I am not the strongest, and I'm sure not the tallest," says Skylar, who is 5 feet 9 inches tall. "I have to be a smart player, and I have to overcompensate with hard work."

A two-time WNBA All-Star starter, Skylar is a starting guard for the Dallas Wings. In 2014, she was the WNBA's Most Improved Player and named to the WNBA First team.

Skylar is also putting her degree to work, diversifying herself across many platforms, from fashion to pop culture and media. As the first female client of Jay Z's Roc Nation Sports, Skylar serves as the face of Nike's Women's Basketball Collection and sponsors Body Armor.

Skylar connects with her young fans through her "Shoot 4 the Sky Basketball Tour," and her Skylar's Scholars program, which highlights the academic achievement of youth who have overcome challenges. She also serves on the board of directors for the GenYouth Foundation.

With a promising future, though, Skylar honors her past, particularly loved ones who invested in her.

Shortly after her graduation from Notre Dame, Skylar's Grandpa Harold passed away.

"He was just an amazing guy, and he was one of my favorite people," Skylar says. "He came to all my games, even when he was sick."

In 2015, after a brilliant start to the WNBA season, Skylar suffered a tear in her right anterior cruciate ligament.

It was her first major injury ever, and she was devastated.

At home, Skylar retreated and reflected.

Skylar's Life Rule

"I realize my family is my foundation," Skylar says. "They all come over to my house and just love on me. 'Are you all taking shifts?' I ask. It's overwhelming. My family make sure I understand that I *always* have a support system. No matter what, we figure things out together."

Skylar's life story is about working hard, believing in yourself, and listening to the voices of encouragement in your life. If you do that, anything is possible.